In Tune With The Infinite

In Tune With The Infinite
By Ralph Waldo Trine

Start Publishing PD LLC
Copyright © 2024 by Start Publishing PD LLC

All rights reserved, including the right to reproduce this book or portions thereof in any form whatsoever.

Start Publishing PD is a registered trademark of Start Publishing PD LLC
Manufactured in the United States of America

Cover art: Shutterstock/Taisiya Kozorez

Cover design: Jennifer Do

10 9 8 7 6 5 4 3 2 1

ISBN 979-8-8809-0598-0

Table of Contents

Introduction 6
A Message From The Author 8
Prelude 11
The Supreme Fact Of The Universe 12
The Supreme Fact Of Human Life 15
Fullness Of Life — Bodily Health And Vigor 26
The Secret, Power And Effects Of Love 46
Wisdom And Interior Illumination 54
The Realization Of Perfect Peace 68
Coming Into Fullness Of Power 75
Plenty Of All Things — The Law Of Prosperity 86
How Men Have Become Prophets, Seers, Sages, And Saviors   94
The Basic Principle Of All Religions
The Universal Religion 98
Entering Now Into The Realization Of The Highest Riches . 102
"The Way" 107
A Resolve For Today 110

Introduction

There is a golden thread that runs through every religion in the world. There is a golden thread that runs through the lives and the teachings to all the prophets, seers, sages, and saviors in the world's history, through the lives of all men of truly great and lasting power. All that they have ever done or attained to has been done in full accordance with law.

What one has done, all may do. This same golden thread must enter into the lives of all who today, in this busy work-a-day world of ours, would exchange impotence for power, weakness and suffering for abounding health and strength pain and unrest for perfect peace, poverty of whatever nature for fullness and plenty.

Each is building their own world. We both build from within and we attract from without. Thought is the force with which we build, for thoughts are forces. Like builds like and like attracts like. In the degree that thought is spiritualized does it become more subtle and powerful in its workings. This spiritualizing is in accordance with law and is within the power of all.

Everything is first worked out in the unseen before it is manifested in the seen, in the ideal before it is realized in the real, in the spiritual before it shows forth in the material. The realm of the unseen is the realm of cause. The realm of the seen is the realm of effect. The nature of effect is always determined and conditioned by the nature of its cause.

To point out the great facts in connection with, and the great laws underlying the workings of the interior, spiritual, thought forces, to point them out so simply and so clearly that even a child can understand, is the author's aim. To point them out so simply and so clearly that all can grasp them, that all can take them and infuse them into everyday life, so as to mold it in all its details in accordance with what they would have it, is his purpose That life can be thus molded by them is not a matter of mere speculation or theory with him, but a matter of positive knowledge

There is a divine sequence running throughout the universe. Within and above and below the human will incessantly works the Divine will. To come into harmony with it and thereby with all the higher laws and forces, to come then into league and to work in conjunction with them, in order that they can work in league and in conjunction with us, is to come into the chain of this wonderful sequence. This is the secret of all success. This is to come into the possession of unknown riches, into the realization of undreamed-of powers.

Within yourself lies the cause of whatever enters into your life. To come into the full realization of your own awakened inner powers is to be able to condition your life in exact accord with what you would have it.

A Message From The Author

we are born into a strange time — a time that tries men's souls. Bewilderment and fear hold many; change and uncertainty stalk through the land — all lands.

Those who keep their courage up and go serenely on are coming through in a way that those who weaken or lie down cannot know. But to do this many lives need help—real concrete help. A remark by an old college friend some years ago has come to my mind every now and then of late. 'After all,' said he, 'it is well for one to have a little philosophy in ones life. A farm boy, eager for a better education and to get ahead pushing his way through college in the face of great odds, he has been doing a splendid work in a great city, and for his country, and yet has always remained humble. His own character indicates to me he has in goodly measure the philosophy which he commended.

'Yes' I replied 'if it has the element of use.' For I had even then read much in the philosophies of the present and of earlier times, and was forced to the conclusion that very large parts of them are of little real value—interesting, but of little real value—because of their lack of the element of use; use in the everyday problems of life.

Each of us has their problems of one sort or another, and no life is free from them. We all need help. This is particularly true at present because of the peculiar time we have been born into.

I have often said to friend and acquaintance during the last two or three years that there is perhaps no one quality men need so much, and right down in their hearts long for so much, as the quality of courage. For courage to me is nothing more or less than a positive, creative type of thought. It not only keeps us going, but all the time works out effects on the course of our journeying. Thoughts are forces, subtle, vital, creative, continually building and shaping our lives according to their nature. It is in this way that the life always and inevitably follows the thought.

Thoughts of strength engender strength from within and attract it from without. Thoughts of weakness actualize weakness within and attract it from without. Courage therefore begets success, as fear begets failure.

There is something in the universe that responds to intrepid thinking. The *power* that holds and that moves the stars in their courses sustains, illumines and fights for the brave and the upright. Courage has power and magic in it. Faith and hope and courage are great producers—we cannot fail if we live always in the brave and cheerful attitude of mind and heart. He alone fails who gives up and lies down.

To open ourselves to this sustaining *Power*, to live continually under its guidance, this is our part. Those of us who do our part will keep free from fear, and therefore from a weakening, corroding worry, the two black twins that carry the germs of despair and defeat, costly for ourselves, unfair for our families, our friends and as our neighbors, costly even for our country.

Years ago, shortly after this book was written, I used on the title page of a little book, as a sort of keynote, the sentence: 'The moment we fully and vitally realize who and what we are, we then begin to build our own world even as God builds His.'

What is the fundamental fact, the fundamental principle of life, the real basis of any healthy or even worthy philosophy of life—Can we find it and know it? There's the rub. But long ago there came one who with a great aptitude for discerning the things of the mind and the spirit, a great clarity of perception that enabled Him to understand the reality of life, the One Life, and to identify His own life with it—the Infinite Spirit of life and power that is back of all, animating and working through all, the life of all.

So direct and intimate was His understanding of it that He used the term Father: I and my Father are one. And to make it of value in that it was not for Him alone, He said: As I am you shall be. My consciousness of the One Life shall be your consciousness, My insight and power shall be your insight and power, if you will receive My message and do the things I tell you. And truly He handled the stuff of life with a wonderful artistry. This is the message that the Master, Jesus of Galilee, tried so hard to get over into the world. It is through this that He becomes the supreme Way-revealer, the Way-revealer to us men of earth.

The Way He showed is what man so sadly needs for a higher and a more efficient individual life, and what the world needs for a more efficient and harmonious and cooperative life. Here is the basis of all idealistic philosophy —a philosophy, a religion of power, of concrete creative power and therefore of use. All are partakers and individual expressions of the One Life, all related and interrelated. As we open ourselves fully to the realization of this we bring harmony into our individual lives, and out of that harmony we create a world of harmony and cooperation, in which each individual and each country enjoys freedom and the fruits of labor, instead of enslavement, of disruption, and of eventual destruction.

Yes, from the conception of the One Life flows the inevitable reality that all men are brothers. There is great gain, there is even an obvious self-interest in building our individual lives and our world life upon that reality. If we do so, we will establish a just and therefore more lasting peace.

What a frightful price we have now to pay for our ignorance, our negligence, our self-seeking, our forgetting that the good of all is the only real and lasting good! Out of all the travail good may come, but again that will depend on us.

We must keep our courage up, must keep our vision clear, must keep our balance, so that we may free ourselves and others with us from the frightful dangers dislocation and disorder that are the results of the great world conflicts.

A single stanza by Edwin Markham voices the poet's inspiration:

At the heart of the cyclone tearing the sky,
And flinging the clouds and the towers by,
Is a place of central calm.
So, here in the roar of mortal things
I have a place where my spirit sings,
In the hollow of God's palm.

This was the poet's way of expressing the great truth we are considering and I know he believed it thoroughly, for we talked it over many times together. This was his belief as to the mission and the revelation of the Master, and the Kingdom of God that comes into being when all men realize they are brothers, and are wise enough to live and to act as brothers.

In this again lie the truth and the song that arose from it and sang itself through our earlier poet Whittier, good Quaker and true always to the "Inner Light":

I know not where His islands lift
Their fronded palms in air,
I only know I cannot drift
Beyond His love and care.

A dark age can come only if we men of earth fail to do our part. We will not fail. We cannot fail. But the sands in the hour-glass may be running lower than we know. We must bestir ourselves.

Prelude

The optimist is right. The pessimist is right. The one differs from the other as the light from the dark. Yet both are right. Each is right from their own particular point of view, and this point of view is the determining factor in the life of each. It determines as to whether it is a life of power or of impotence, of peace or of pain, of success or of failure.

The optimist has the power of seeing things in their entirety and in their right relations. The pessimist looks from a limited and a one-sided point of view. The one has their understanding illuminated by wisdom, the understanding of the other is darkened by ignorance. Each is building their world from within, and the result of the building are determined by the point of view of each The optimist, by their superior wisdom and insight, is making their own heaven, and in the degree that they make their own heaven are helping to make one for all the world beside. The pessimist, by virtue of their limitations, are making their own hell, and in the degree that they make their own hell are they helping to make one for all mankind.

You and I have the predominating characteristics of an optimist or the predominating characteristics of a pessimist. We then are making, hour by hour, our own heaven or our own hell; and in the degree that we are making the one or the other for ourselves are we helping make it for all the world beside.

The word heaven means harmony. The word hell is from the Old English hell, meaning to build a wall around, to separate; to be helled was to be shut off from. Now if there is such a thing as harmony there must be that something one can be in right relations with; for to be in right relations with anything is to be in harmony with it. Again, if there is such a thing as being helled, shut off, separated from, there must be that something from which one is helled, shut off, or separated.

The Supreme Fact Of The Universe

The great central fact of the universe is that Spirit of Infinite Life and Power that is behind all, that animates all, that manifests itself in and through all; that self-existent principle of life from which all has come, and not only from which all has come, but from which all is continually coming. If there is an individual life, there must of necessity be an infinite source of life from which it comes. If there is a quality or a force of love, there must of necessity be an infinite source of love whence it comes. If there is wisdom, there must be the all-wise source behind it from which it springs. The same is true in regard to peace, the same in regard to power, the same in regard to what we call material things.

There is then this Spirit of Infinite Life and Power behind all, which is the source of all. This Infinite Power is creating, working, ruling through the agency of great immutable laws and forces that run through all the universe that surrounds us on every side. Every act of our everyday lives is governed by these same great laws and forces. Every flower that blooms by the wayside, springs up, grows, blooms, fades, according to certain great immutable laws. Every snowflake that plays between earth and heaven, forms, falls, melts, according to certain great unchangeable laws.

In a sense there is nothing in all the great universe but law. If this is true there must of necessity be a force behind it all that is maker of these laws, and a force greater than the laws that are made. This Spirit of Infinite Life and Power that is behind all is what I call God. I care not what term you may use, be it Kindly Light, Providence, the Over Soul, Omnipotence, or whatever term may be most convenient. I care not what the term may be as long as we are agreed in regard to the great central fact itself.

God, then, is this Infinite Spirit which fills all the universe with Himself alone, so that all is from Him and in Him, and there is nothing that is outside. Indeed and in truth, then, in Him we live and move and have our being. He is the life of our life, our very life itself. We have received, we are continually receiving our life from Him. We are partakers of the life of God; and though we differ from Him in that we are individualized spirits, while He is the Spirit including us as well as all else beside, yet in essence the life of God and the life of man are identically the same, and so are one. They differ not in essence, in quality; they differ in degree.

There have been and are highly illumined souls who believe we receive our life from God after the manner of a divine inflow. And again, there have been and are those who believe that our life is one with the life of God, and so that God and man are one. Which is right? Both are right; both right when rightly understood.

In regard to the first: if God is the Infinite Spirit of Life behind all, whence all comes, then clearly our life as individualized spirits is continually coming from this infinite Source by means of this divine inflow. In the second place, if our lives as individualized spirits are directly from, are parts of this Infinite Spirit of Life, then the degree of the Infinite Spirit that is manifested in the life of each be identical in quality with that Source, just as a drop of water from the ocean is, in nature, in characteristics, identical with the ocean, its source. And how could it be otherwise? The liability to misunderstanding in this latter case, however, is this: in that although the life of God and the life of man in essence are identically the same, the life of God so far transcends the life of individual man that it includes all else beside. In other words, so far as the quality of life is concerned, in essence they are the same so far as the degree of life is concerned they are vastly different.

In this light is it not then evident that both conceptions are true, and, more, that they are one and the same? Both conceptions may be typified by one and the same illustration.

There is a reservoir in a valley which receives its supply from an inexhaustible reservoir on the mountain side. It is then true that the reservoir in the valley receives its supply by virtue of the inflow of the water from the larger reservoir on the mountain side. It is also true that the water in this smaller reservoir is in nature, in quality, in characteristics identically the same as that in the larger reservoir which is its source. The difference, however, is this: the reservoir on the mountain side, in the amount of its water, so far transcends the reservoir in the valley that it can supply an innumerable number of like reservoirs and still be unexhausted.

And so in the life of man. If, as I think we have already agreed, however we may differ in regard to anything else, there is this Infinite Spirit of Life behind all, the life of all, and so, from which all comes, then the life of individual man, your life and mine, must come by a divine inflow from this Infinite Source, And if this is true then the life that comes by this inflow to man is necessarily the same in essence as is this Infinite Spirit of Life. There is a difference. It is not a difference in essence. It is a difference in degree.

If this is true, does it not then follow that in the degree that man opens himself to this divine inflow does he approach to God? If so, it then necessarily follows that in the degree that he makes this approach does he take on the God-powers. And if the God-powers are without limit, does it not then follow that the only limitations are the limitations he sets to himself, by virtue of not knowing himself?

The Supreme Fact Of Human Life

From the great central fact of the universe in regard to which we have agreed? namely, this Spirit of Infinite Life that is behind all and from which all comes, we are led to inquire as to what is the great central fact in human life. From what has gone before, the question almost answers itself.

The great central fact in human life, in your life and mine, is the coming into a conscious, vital realization of our oneness with this Infinite Life, and the opening of ourselves fully to this divine inflow.

This is the great central fact in human life, for in this all else is included, all else follows in its train. In just the degree that we come into a conscious realization of our oneness with the Infinite Life, and open ourselves to this divine inflow, do we actualize in ourselves the qualities and powers of the Infinite Life.

And what does this mean? It means simply this: that we are recognizing our true identity, that we are bringing our lives into harmony with the same great laws and forces, and so opening ourselves to the same great inspirations, as have all the prophets, seers, sages, and saviors in the world's history, all men of truly great and mighty power. For in the degree that we come into this realization and connect ourselves with this Infinite Source, do we make it possible for the higher powers to play, to work, to manifest through us.

We keep closed to this divine inflow, to these higher forces and powers, through ignorance, as most of us do, and thus hinder or even prevent their manifesting through us. Or we can intentionally close ourselves to their operations and thus deprive ourselves of the powers to which, by the very nature of our being, we are rightful heirs. On the other hand, we can come into so vital a realization of the oneness of our real selves with this Infinite Life, and can open ourselves so fully to the incoming of this divine inflow, and so the operation of these higher forces, inspirations, and powers, that we can indeed and in truth become what we may well term, God-men.

And what is a God-man? One in whom the powers of God are manifesting, though yet a man. No one can set limitations to a man of this type, for the only limitations he can have are those set by the self. Ignorance is the most potent factor in setting limitations to the majority of mankind, and so the great majority of people continue to live their little, dwarfed, and stunted lives simply by virtue of the fact that they do not realize the larger life to which they are heirs. They have never as yet come into a knowledge of the real identity of their true selves.

Mankind has not yet realized that the real self is one with the life of God. Through its ignorance it has never yet opened itself to the divine inflow, and so has never made itself a channel through which the infinite powers and forces can manifest. When we know ourselves merely as men, we live accordingly, and have the powers of men. When we come into the realization of the fact that we are God-men, then again we live accordingly, and have the powers of God-men. In the degree that we open ourselves to this divine inflow are we changed from mere men into God-men.

A friend has a beautiful lotus pond. A natural basin on his estate —his farm as he always calls it —is supplied with water from a reservoir in the foothills some distance away. A gate regulates the flow of the water from the main that conducts it from the reservoir to the pond. It is a spot of transcendent beauty. There, through the days of the perfect summer weather, the lotus flowers lie full blown upon the surface of the clear, transparent water. The June roses and other wild flowers are continually blooming upon its banks. The birds come here to drink and bathe, and from early until late one can hear the melody of their song. The bees are continually at work in this garden of wild flowers. A beautiful grove, in which many kinds of wild berries and many varieties of brakes and ferns grow, stretches at the back of the pond as far as the eye can reach.

Our friend is a man, nay more, a God-man, a lover of his kind, and as a consequence no notice bearing such words as 'Private rounds, no trespassing allowed,' or Trespassers will be prosecuted,' stands on his estate. But at the end of a beautiful by-way that leads through the wildwood up to this enchanting spot, stands a notice bearing the words 'All are welcome to the Lotus Pond.' All love our friend. Why? They can't help it. He so loves them, and what is his is theirs.

Here one may often find merry groups of children at play. Here many times tired and weary-looking men come, and somehow, when they go their faces wear a different expression —the burden seems to be lifted, and now and then I have heard them when leaving, sometimes in a faint murmur, as if uttering a benediction, say, 'God bless our brother-friend.' Many speak of this spot as the Garden of God. My friend calls it his Soul Garden, and he spends many hours in quiet here. Often have I seen him after the others have gone, walking to and fro, or sitting quietly in the clear moonlight on an old rustic bench, drinking in the perfume of the wild flowers. He is a man of a beautifully simple nature. He says that here his greatest and most successful plans, many times as by a flash of inspiration, suggest themselves to him.

Everything in the immediate vicinity seems to breathe a spirit of kindliness, comfort, goodwill, and good cheer. The very cattle and sheep as they come to the old stone-fence at the edge of the grove and look across to this beautiful spot seem, indeed, to get the same enjoyment that the people are getting. They seem almost to smile in the realization of their contentment and enjoyment, or perhaps it seems so to the looker-on, because he can scarcely help smiling as he sees the manifested evidence of their contentment and pleasure.

The gate of the pond is always open wide enough to admit a supply of water so abundant that it continually overflows a quantity sufficient to feed a stream that runs through the fields below, giving the pure mountain water in drink to the cattle and flocks that are grazing there. The stream then flows on through the neighbor's fields.

Not long ago our friend was absent for a year. He rented his estate during his absence to a man who, as the world goes, was of a very 'practical' turn of mind. He had no time for anything that did not bring him direct practical returns. The gate connecting the reservoir with the lotus pond was shut down, and no longer had the crystal mountain water the opportunity to feed and overflow it. The notice of our friend, 'All are welcome to the Lotus Pond,' was removed, and no longer were the gay companies of children and of men seen at the pond. A great change came over everything. On account of the lack of the life-giving water the flowers in the pond wilted, and their long stems lay stretched upon the mud in the bottom. The fish that formerly swam in its clear water soon died and gave off an offensive odor to all who came near. The flowers no longer bloomed on its banks. The birds no longer came to drink and to bathe. No longer was heard the hum of the bees, and more, the stream that ran through the fields below dried up, so that the cattle and the flocks no longer got their supply of clear mountain water.

The difference between the spot now and the lotus pond when our friend gave it his careful attention was caused, as we readily see, by the shutting of the gate to the pond, thus preventing the water from the reservoir in the hills, which was the source of its life, from entering it. And when this, the source of its life, was shut off, not only was the appearance of the lotus pond entirely changed, but the surrounding fields were deprived of the stream to whose banks the flocks and cattle came for drink.

In this do we not see a complete parallel so far as human life is concerned? In the degree that we recognize our oneness, our connection with the Infinite Spirit which is the life of all, and in the degree that we open ourselves to this divine inflow, do we come into harmony with the highest, the most powerful, and the most beautiful everywhere. And in the degree that we do this do we overflow, so that all who come in contact with us receive the effects of this realization on our part. This is the lotus pond of our friend, he who is in love with all that is truest and best in the universe. And in the degree that we fail to recognize our oneness with this Infinite Source, and so close, shut ourselves to this divine inflow, do we come into that state where there seems to be with us nothing of good, nothing of beauty, nothing of power, and when this is true, those who come in contact with us receive not good, but harm. This is the spot of the lotus pond while the farm was in the hands of a tenant.

There is this difference between the lotus pond and your life and mine. It has no power in itself of opening the gate to the inflow of the water from the reservoir which is its source. In regard to this it is helpless, and dependent upon an outside agency. You and I have the power, the power within us, to open or close ourselves to this divine inflow exactly as we choose. This we have through the power or mind through the operation of thought.

There is the soul of life, direct from God. This it is that relates us to the Infinite. There is, then, the physical life. This it is that relates us to the material universe about us. The thought life connects the one with the other. It is this that plays between the two.

Before we proceed further let us consider very briefly the nature of thought. Thought is not, as is many times supposed, a mere indefinite abstraction, or something of a like nature. It is, on the contrary, a vital, living force, the most vital, subtle, and irresistible force there is in the universe.

In our very laboratory experiments we are demonstrating the great fact that thoughts are forces. They have form, and quality, and substance, and power, and we are beginning to find that there is what we may term a science of thought. We are beginning also to find that through the instrumentality of our thought forces we have creative power not merely in a figurative sense, but creative power in reality.

Everything in the material universe about us, everything the universe has ever known, had its origin first in thought. From this it took its form. Every castle, every statue, every painting, every piece of mechanism, everything had its birth, its origin, first in the mind of the one who formed it before it received its material expression or embodiment. The very universe in which we live is the result of the thought energies of God, the Infinite Spirit that is behind all. And if it is true, as we have found, that we in our true selves are in essence the same, and in this sense are one with the life of this Infinite Spirit, do we not then see that in the degree that we come into a vital realization of this stupendous fact, we, through the operation of our interior, spiritual, thought forces, have in like sense creative power?

Everything exists in the unseen before it is manifested or realized in the seen, and in this sense it is true that the unseen things are the real, while the things that are seen are the unreal. The unseen things are the cause, the seen things are effect. The unseen things are the eternal the seen things are the changing, the transient. The 'power of the word' is a literal scientific fact. Through the operation of our thought forces we have creative power. The spoken word is nothing more or less than the outward expression of the workings of these interior forces. The spoken word is then, in a sense, the means whereby the thought forces are focused and directed along any particular line, and this concentration, this giving them direction, is necessary before any outward or material manifestation of their power can become evident.

Much is said in regard to building castles in the air, and one who is given to this building is not always looked upon with favor. But castles in the air are always necessary before we can have castles on the ground, before we can have castles in which to live. The trouble with the one who gives himself to building castles in the air is not that he builds them in the air, but that he does not go farther and actualize in life, in character, in material form, the castles he thus builds. He does a part of the work, a very necessary part, but another equally necessary part remains still undone.

There is in connection with the thought forces what we may term the drawing power of mind, and the great law operating here is one with the great law of the universe, that like attracts like. We are continually attracting to us, from both the seen and the unseen side of life, forces and conditions most akin to those of our own thoughts.

This law is continually operating whether we are conscious of it or not. We are all living, so to speak, in a vast ocean of thought, and the very atmosphere around us is continually filled with the thought forces that are being continually sent or that are continually going out in the form of thought waves. We are all affected, more or less, by these thought forces, either consciously or unconsciously and in the degree that we are more or less sensitively organized, or in the degree that we are negative and so are open to outside influences, rather than positive, thus determining what influences shall enter into our realm of thought, and hence into our lives.

There are those among us who are much more sensitively organized than others. As an organism their bodies are more finely, more sensitively constructed. These, generally speaking, are people who are always more or less affected by the mentalities of those with whom they come in contact, or in whose company they are. A friend, the editor of one of our great journals, is so sensitively organized that it is impossible for him to attend a gathering, such as a reception, talk and shake hands with a number of people during the course of the evening, without taking on, to a greater or less extent, their various mental and physical conditions. These affect him to such an extent that he is scarcely himself, and in his best condition for work, until some two or three days afterwards.

Some think it unfortunate for one to be sensitively organized. By no means. It is a good thing, for one may thus be more open and receptive to the higher impulses of the soul within, and to all higher forces and influences from without. It may, however, be unfortunate and extremely inconvenient to be so organized unless one recognize and gain the power of closing themselves, of making themselves positive to all detrimental or undesirable influences. This power everyone, however sensitively organized they may be, can acquire.

This they can acquire through the mind's action. And, moreover, there is no habit of more value to anyone, be they sensitively or less sensitively organized, than that of occasionally taking and holding themselves continually in the attitude of mind — I close myself, I make myself positive to all things below, and open and receptive to higher influences, to all things above. By taking this attitude of mind consciously now and then it soon becomes a habit, and if one is deeply in earnest in regard to it, it puts into operation silent but subtle and powerful influences in effecting the desired results. In this way all lower and undesirable influences from both the seen and the unseen side of life are closed out, while all higher influences are invited, and in the degree that they are invited will they enter.

And what do we mean by the unseen side of life? First, the thought forces, the mental and emotional conditions in the atmosphere about us that are generated by those manifesting on the physical plane through the agency of physical bodies. Second, the same forces generated by those who have dropped the physical body, or from whom it has been struck away, and who are now manifesting through the agency of bodies of a different nature.

The individual existence of man begins on the sense plane of the physical world, but rises through successive gradations of ethereal and celestial spheres, corresponding with his ever unfolding deific life and powers, to a destiny of unspeakable grandeur and glory. Within and above every physical planet is a corresponding ethereal planet, or soul world, as within and above every physical organism is a corresponding ethereal organism, or soul body, of which the physical is but the external counterpart and materialized expression.

From this etherealized or soul planet, which is the immediate home of our arisen humanity, there rises or deepens in infinite gradations spheres within and above spheres, to celestial heights of spiritualized existence utterly inconceivable to the sense of man. Embodiment, accordingly, is two-fold —the physical being but the temporary husk, so to speak, in and by which the real and permanent ethereal organism is individualized and perfected, somewhat as 'the full corn in the ear' is reached by means of its husk, for which there is no further use. By means of this indestructible ethereal body the corresponding ethereal spheres of environment with the social life and relations in the spheres, the individuality and personal life is preserved forever.'

The fact of life in whatever form means the continuance of life, even though the form be changed. Life is the one eternal principle of the universe and so always continues, even though the form of the agency through which it manifests be changed. 'In My Father's house are many mansions.' And, surely, because the individual has dropped, has gone out of the physical body, there is no evidence at all that the life does not go right on the same as before, not commencing for there is no cessation but commencing in the other form exactly where it has left off here, for all life is a continuous evolution, step by step, there one neither skips nor jumps.

There are in the other form, then, mentalities and hence lives of all grades and influences, just as there are in the physical form. If, then, the great law that like attracts like is ever operating, we are continually attracting to us from this side of life influences and conditions most akin to those of our own thoughts and lives. A gruesome thought that we should be so influenced, says one. By no means, all life is one, we are all bound together in the one common and universal life. Especially not so when we take into consideration the fact that we have it entirely in our own hands to determine the order of thought we entertain, and consequently the order of influences we attract, and are not mere willowy creatures of circumstance, unless indeed we choose to be.

In our mental lives we can either keep hold of the rudder and so determine exactly what course we take, what points we touch, or we can fail to do this, and failing, we drift, and are blown hither and thither by every passing breeze. And so, on the contrary, welcome should be the thought, for thus we may draw to us the influence and the aid of the greatest, the noblest, and the best who have lived on the earth, whatever the time, wherever the place.

We cannot rationally believe other than that those who have labored in love and with uplifting power here are still laboring in the same way, and in all probability with more earnest zeal, and with still greater power.

'And Elisha prayed, and said, Lord, I pray thee, open his eyes, that he may see. And the Lord opened the eyes of the young man, and he saw: and, behold, the mountain was full of horses and chariots of fire round about Elisha.'

While riding with a friend a few days ago, we were speaking of the great interest people are everywhere taking in the more vital things of life, the eagerness with which they are reaching out for a knowledge of the interior forces, their ever-increasing desire to know themselves and to know their true relations with the Infinite. And in speaking of the great spiritual awakening that is so rapidly coming all over the world, the beginnings of which we are so clearly seeing during the closing years of this, and whose ever-increasing proportions we are to witness during the early years of the coming century, I said, 'How beautiful if Emerson, the illumined one so far in advance of his time, who labored so faithfully and so fearlessly to bring about these very conditions, how beautiful if he were with us today to witness it all! how he would rejoice!' 'How do we know', was the reply, 'that he is not witnessing it all? and more, that he is not having a hand in it all —a hand even greater, perhaps, than when we saw him here?' Thank you, my friend, for this reminder. And, truly, 'are they not all ministering spirits sent forth to minister to those who shall be heirs of salvation?'

As science is so abundantly demonstrating today, the things that we see are but a very small fraction of the things that are. The real, vital forces at work in our own lives and in the world about us are not seen by the ordinary physical eye. Yet they are the causes of which all things we see are merely the effects. Thoughts are forces, like builds like, and like attracts like. For one to govern their thinking, then, is to determine their life.

Says one of deep insight into the nature of things, 'The law of correspondences between spiritual and material things is wonderfully exact in its workings. People ruled by the mood of gloom attract to them gloomy things. People always discouraged and despondent do not succeed in anything, and live only by burdening someone else. The hopeful, confident, and cheerful attract the elements of success. A man's front or back garden will advertise that man's ruling mood in the way it is kept. A woman at home shows her state of mind in her dress.

A slattern advertises the ruling mood of hopelessness, carelessness, and lack of system. Rags, tatters, and dirt are always in the mind before being on the body. The thought that is most put out brings its corresponding visible element to crystallize about you as surely and literally as the visible bit of copper in solution attracts to it the invisible copper in that solution. A mind always hopeful, confident, courageous, and determined on its set purpose, and keeping itself to that purpose, attracts to itself out of the elements things and powers favorable to that purpose.

'Every thought of yours has a literal value to you in every possible way. The strength of your body, the strength of your mind, your success in business, and the pleasure your company brings others, depends on the nature of your thoughts...... In whatever mood you set your mind does your spirit receive of unseen substance in correspondence with that mood. It is as much a chemical law as a spiritual law. Chemistry is not confined to the elements we see. The elements we do not see with the physical eye outnumber ten thousand times those we do see.

The Christ injunction, "Do good to those who hate you," is based on a scientific fact and a natural law. So, to do good is to bring to yourself all the elements in nature of power and good. To do evil is to bring the contrary destructive elements. When our eyes are opened, self-preservation will make us stop all evil thought. Those who live by hate will die of hate: that is, "those who live by the sword will die by the sword." Every evil thought is as a sword drawn on the person to whom it is directed. If a sword is drawn in return, so much the worse for both.'

And says another who knows full well whereof he speaks: 'The law of attraction works universally on every plane of action, and we attract whatever we desire or expect. If we desire one thing and expect another, we become like houses divided against themselves, which are quickly brought to desolation. Determine resolutely to expect only what you desire, then you will attract only what you wish for. . . . Carry any kind of thought you please about with you, and so long as you retain it, no matter how you roam over land or sea, you will unceasingly attract to yourself, knowingly or inadvertently, exactly and only what corresponds to your own dominant quality of thought. Thoughts are our private property, and we can regulate them to suit our taste entirely by steadily recognizing our ability so to do.'

We have just spoken of the drawing power of mind. Faith is nothing more nor less than the operation of the thought forces in the form of an earnest desire, coupled with expectation as to its fulfillment. And in the degree that faith, the earnest desire thus sent out, is continually held to and watered by firm expectation, in just that degree does it either draw to itself, or does it change from the unseen into the visible, from the spiritual into the material, that for which it is sent.

Let the element of doubt or fear enter in, and what would otherwise be a tremendous force will be so neutralized that it will fail of its realization. Continually held to and continually watered by firm expectation, it becomes a force, a drawing power, that is irresistible and absolute, and the results will be absolute in direct proportion as it is absolute.

We shall find, as we are so rapidly beginning to find today, that the great things said in regard to faith, the great promises made in connection with it, are not mere vague sentimentalities, but are all great scientific facts, and rest upon great immutable laws. Even in our very laboratory experiments we are beginning to discover the laws underlying and governing these forces. We are now beginning, some at least, to use them understandingly and not blindly, as has so often and so long been the case.

Much is said today in regard to the will. It is many times spoken of as if it were a force in itself. But will is a force, a power, only in so far as it is a particular form of the manifestation of the thought forces, for it is by what we call the 'will' that thought is focused and given a particular direction, and in the degree that thought is thus focused and given direction, is it effective in the work it is sent out to accomplish.

In a sense there are two kinds of will—the human and the divine. The human will is the will of what, for convenience sake, we may term the lower self. It is the will that finds its life merely in the realm of the mental and the physical—the sense will. It is the will of the one who is not yet awake to the fact that there is a life that far transcends the life of merely the intellect and the physical senses, and which, when realized and lived, does not do away with or minify these, but which, on the contrary, brings them to their highest perfection and to their powers of keenest enjoyment. The divine will is the will of the higher self, the will of the one who recognizes their oneness with the Divine, and who consequently brings their will to work in harmony, in conjunction with the divine a will. 'The Lord thy God in the midst of thee is mighty.'

The human will has its limitations. So far and no farther, says the law. The divine will has no limitations. It is supreme. All things are open and subject to you, says the law, and so, in the degree that the human will is transmuted into the divine, in the degree that it comes into harmony with, and so acts in conjunction with the divine, does it become supreme. Then it is that 'Thou shalt decree a thing and it shall be established unto thee.' The great secret of life and power, then, is to make and to keep one's conscious connection with this Infinite Source.

The power of every life, the very life itself, is determined by what it relates itself to. God is immanent as well as transcendent. He is creating, working, ruling in the universe today, in your life and in mine, just as much as He ever has been. We are apt to regard Him after the manner of an absentee landlord, one who has set into operation the forces of this great universe, and then taken Himself away.

In the degree, however, that we recognized Him as immanent as well as transcendent, are we able to partake of His life and power. For in the degree that we recognize Him as the Infinite Spirit of Life and Power that is today, at this very moment, working and manifesting in and through all, and then, in the degree that we come into realization of our oneness with this life, do we become partakers of, and so do we actualize in ourselves the qualities of His Life. In the degree that we open ourselves to the inflowing tide of this immanent and transcendent life, do we make ourselves channels through which the Infinite Intelligence and Power can work.

It is through the instrumentality of the mind that we are enabled to connect the real soul life with the physical life, and so enable the soul life to manifest and work through the physical. The thought life needs continually to be illumined from within. This illumination can come in just the degree that through the agency of the mind we recognize our oneness with the Divine, of which each soul is an individual form of expression.

This gives us the inner guiding which we call intuition. 'Intuition is to the spiritual nature and understanding practically what sense perception is to the sensuous nature and understanding. It is an inner spiritual sense through which man is opened to the direct revelation and knowledge of God, the secrets of nature and life, and through which he is brought into conscious unity and fellowship with God, and made to realize his own deific nature and supremacy of being as the son of God. Spiritual supremacy and illumination, thus realized through the development and perfection of intuition under divine inspiration, gives the perfect inner vision and direct insight into the character, properties, and purpose of all things to which the attention and interest are directed.....

It is we repeat, a spiritual sense opening inwardly, as the physical senses open outwardly, and because it has the capacity to perceive, grasp and know the truth at first hand, independent of all external sources of information, we call it intuition. All inspired teaching and spiritual revelations are based upon the recognition of this spiritual faculty of the soul, and its power to receive and appropriate them...... Conscious unity of man in spirit and purpose with the Father, born out of his supreme desire and trust, opens his soul through this inner sense to immediate inspiration and enlightenment from the Divine Omniscience, and the cooperative energy of the Divine Omnipotence, under which he becomes a seer and a master.

'On this higher plane of realized spiritual life in the flesh the mind holds the impersonal attitude and acts with unfettered freedom and unbiased vision, grasping truth at first hand, independent of all external sources of information. Approaching all beings and things from the divine side, they are seen in the light of the divine Omniscience. God's purpose in them, and so the truth concerning them, as it rests in the mind of God, are thus revealed by direct illumination from the Divine Mind, to which the soul is opened inwardly through this spiritual sense we call intuition.' Some call it the voice of the soul, some call it the voice of God, some call it the sixth sense. It is our inner spiritual sense.

In the degree that we come into the recognition of our own true selves, into the realization of the oneness of our life with the Infinite Life, and in the degree that we open ourselves to this divine inflow, does this voice of intuition, this voice of the soul, this voice of God, speak clearly, and in the degree that we recognize, listen to, and obey it, does it speak ever more clearly, until by-and-by there comes the time when it is unerring, absolutely unerring, in its guidance.

Fullness Of Life — Bodily Health And Vigor

God is the Spirit of Infinite Life. If we are partakers of this life and have the power of opening ourselves fully to its divine inflow, it means more, so far to its divine inflow, it means more, so far as even the physical life is concerned, than we may at first think. For very clearly, the life of this Infinite Spirit, from its very nature, can admit of no disease, and if this is true, no disease can exist in the body where it freely enters, through which it freely flows.

Let us recognize at the outset that, so far as the physical life is concerned, all life is from within outwards. There is an immutable law which says: 'As within, so without, cause, effect.' In other words, the thought forces, the various mental states and the emotions, all have in time their effects upon the physical body.

Someone says, 'I hear a great deal said today in regard to the effects of the mmd upon the body, but I don't know that I place very much confidence in this.' Don't you? Someone brings you sudden news. You grow pale, you tremble, or perhaps you fall into a faint. It is, however, through the channel of your mind that the news is imparted to you. A friend says something to you, perhaps at the table, something that seems very unkind. You are hurt by it as we say. You have been enjoying your dinner, but from this moment your appetite is gone. But what was said entered into and affected you through the channel of your mind.

Look! Yonder goes a young man, dragging his feet, stumbling over the slightest obstruction in the path. Why is it? Simply that he is weak-minded, an idiot. In other words, a falling state of mind is productive of a falling condition of the body. To be sure-minded is to be sure footed. To be uncertain in mind is to be uncertain in step.

Again, a sudden emergency arises. You stand trembling and weak with fear. Why are you powerless to move? Why do you tremble? And yet you believe that the mind has but little influence upon the body. You are for a moment dominated by a fit of anger. For a few hours afterwards you complain of a violent headache. And still you do not seem to realize that the thoughts and emotions have an effect upon the body.

A day or two ago, while conversing with a friend, we were speaking of worry. 'My father is greatly given to worry,' he said. 'Your father is not a healthy man' I said. 'He is not strong, vigorous, robust, and active.' I then went on to describe to him more fully his father's condition and the troubles which afflicted him. He looked at me in surprise and said, 'Why, you do not know my father?' 'No,' I replied. 'How then can you describe so accurately the disease with which he is afflicted?' 'You have just told me that your father is greatly given to worry. When you told me this you indicated to me cause. In describing your father's condition I simply connected with the cause its own peculiar effects.'

Fear and worry have the effect of closing up the channels of the body, so that the life forces flow in a slow and sluggish manner. Hope and tranquility open the channels of the body, so that the life forces go bounding through it in such a way that disease can rarely get a foothold.

Not long ago a lady was telling a friend of a serious physical trouble. My friend happened to know that between this lady and her sister the most kindly relations did not exist. He listened attentively to her delineation of her troubles, and then, looking her squarely in the face, in a firm but kindly tone, said: 'Forgive your sister.' The woman looked at him in surprise and said: 'I can't forgive my sister' 'Very well, then,' he replied, 'keep the stiffness of your joints and your kindred rheumatic troubles.'

A few weeks later he saw her again. With a light step she came toward him and said I took your advice. I saw my sister and forgave her. We have become good friends again, and I don't know how it is, but somehow or other from the very day, as I remember, that we became reconciled, my troubles seemed to grow less and today there is not a trace of the old difficulties left, and really, my sister and I have become such good friends that now we can scarcely get along without one another.' Again we have effect following cause.

We have several well-authenticated cases of the following nature. A mother has been dominated for a few moments by an intense passion of anger, and the child at her breast has died within an hour's time, so poisoned became the mother's milk by virtue of the poisonous secretions of the system while under the domination of this fit of anger. In other cases it has caused severe illness and convulsions.

The following experiment has been tried a number of times by a well-known scientist. Several men have been put into a heated room. Each man has been dominated for a moment by a particular passion of some kind, one by an intense passion of anger, and others by different other passions. The experimenter has taken a drop of perspiration from the body of each of these men, and by means of a careful chemical analysis he has been able to determine the particular passion by which each has been dominated. Practically the same results revealed themselves in the chemical analysis of the saliva of each of the men.

Says a noted American author, an able graduate of a great medical school and one who has studied deeply into the forces that build the body and the forces that tear it down: 'The mind is the natural protector of the body..... Every thought tends to reproduce itself, and ghastly mental pictures of disease, sensuality, and vice of all sorts, produce scrofula and leprosy in the soul, which reproduces them in the body. Anger changes the chemical properties of the saliva to a poison dangerous to life. It is well known that sudden and violent emotions have not only weakened the heart in a few hours, but have caused death and insanity.

It has been discovered by scientists that there is a chemical difference between that sudden cold exudation of a person under a deep sense of guilt and the ordinary perspiration, and the state of the mind can sometimes be determined by chemical analysis of the perspiration of a criminal, which, when brought into contact with selenic acid, produces a distinctive pink color. It is well known that fear has killed thousands of victims, while, on the other hand, courage is a great invigorator.

'Anger in the mother may poison a nursing child. Rarey, the celebrated horse-tamer, said that an angry word would sometimes raise the pulse of a horse ten beats in a minute. If this is true of a beast, what can we say of its power upon human beings, especially upon a child? Strong mental emotion often causes vomiting. Extreme anger or fright may produce jaundice. A violent paroxysm of rage has caused apoplexy and death. Indeed, in more than one instance, a single night of mental agony has wrecked a life. Grief, long-standing jealousy, constant care and corroding anxiety sometimes tend to develop insanity. Sick thoughts and discordant moods are the natural atmosphere of disease, and crime is engendered and thrives in the miasma of the mind.'

From all this we get the great fact we are scientifically demonstrating today that the various mental states, emotions, and passions have their various peculiar effects upon the body, and each induces in turn, if indulged in to any great extent, its own peculiar forms of disease, and these in time become chronic.

Just a word or two in regard to their mode of operation. If a person is dominated for a moment by, say, a passion of anger, there is set up in the physical organism what we might justly term a bodily thunder-storm, which has the effect of souring, or rather of corroding, the normal, healthy, and life-giving secretions of the body, so that instead of performing their natural functions they become poisonous and destructive. And if this goes on to any great extent by virtue of their cumulative influences they give rise to a particular form of disease, which in turn becomes chronic. So the emotion opposite to this, that of kindliness, love, benevolence, goodwill, tends to stimulate a healthy, purifying, and life-giving flow of all the bodily secretions. All the channels of the body seem free and open, the life forces go bounding through them. And these very forces, set into a bounding activity, will in time counteract the poisonous and disease-giving effects of their opposites.

A physician goes to see a patient. He gives no medicine this morning. Yet the very fact of his going makes the patient better. He has carried with him the spirit of health, he has carried brightness of tone and disposition, he has carried hope into the sick chamber, he has left it there. In fact, the very hope and good cheer he has carried with him has taken hold of and has had a subtle but powerful influence upon the mind of the patient, and this mental condition imparted by the physician has in turn its effects upon the patient's body, and so through the instrumentality of this mental suggestion the healing goes on.

> Know, then, whatever cheerful and serene
> Supports the mind, supports the body, too.
> Hence the most vital movement mortals feel
> Is hope, the balm and life-blood of the soul.

We sometimes hear a person in weak health say to another, 'I always feel better when you come.' There is a deep scientific reason underlying the statement. 'The tongue of the wise is health.' The power of suggestion so far as the human mind is concerned is a most wonderful and interesting field of study. Most wonderful and powerful forces can be set into operation through this agency. One of the world's most noted scientists, recognized everywhere as one of the most eminent anatomists living, tells us that he has proved from laboratory experiments that the entire human structure can be completely changed, made over, within a period of less than one year, and that some portions can be entirely remade within a period of a very few weeks.

'Do you mean to say,' I hear it asked, 'that the body can be changed from a diseased to a healthy condition through the operation of the interior forces?' Most certainly, and more, this is the natural method of cure. The method that has as its work the application of drugs, medicines and external agencies is the artificial method. The only thing that any drug or any medicine can do is to remove obstructions, that the life forces may have simply a better chance to do their work. The real healing process must be performed by the operation of the life forces within.

A surgeon and physician of worldwide fame recently made to his medical associates the following declaration: 'For generations past the most important influence that plays upon nutrition, the life principle itself, has remained an unconsidered element in the medical profession, and the almost exclusive drift of its studies and remedial paraphernalia has been confined to the action of matter over mind.

This has seriously interfered with the evolutionary tendencies of the doctors themselves, and consequently the psychic factor in professional life is still in a rudimentary or comparatively undeveloped state. But the light of the nineteenth century has dawned, and so the march of mankind in general is taken in the direction of the hidden forces of nature. Doctors are now compelled to join the ranks of students in psychology and follow their patrons into the broader field of mental therapeutics. There is no time for lingering, no time for skepticism or doubt or hesitation. He who lingers is lost, for the entire race is enlisted in the movement.'

I am aware of the fact that in connection with the matter we are now considering there has been a great deal of foolishness during recent years. Many absurd and foolish things have been claimed and done; but this says nothing against, and it has absolutely nothing to do with the great underlying laws themselves. The same has been true of the early days of practically every system of ethics or philosophy or religion the world has ever known. But as time has passed, these foolish, absurd things have fallen away, and the great eternal principles have stood out ever more and more clearly defined.

I know personally of many cases where an entire and permanent cure has been effected, in some within a remarkably short period of time, through the operation of these forces. Some of them are cases that had been entirely given up by the regular practice, materia medica. We have numerous accounts of such cases in all times and in connection with all religions. And why should not the power of effecting such cures exist among us today? The power does exist, and it will be actualized in just the degree that we recognize the same great laws that were recognized in times past.

One person may do a very great deal in connection with the healing of another, but this almost invariably implies cooperation on the part of the one who is thus treated. In the cures that Christ performed He almost always needed the cooperation of the one who appealed to Him. His question almost invariably was, 'Dost thou believe?' He thus stimulated into activity the life-giving forces within the one cured. If one is in a very weak condition, or if their nervous system is exhausted, or if their mind through the influence of the disease is not so strong in its workings, it may be well for them for a time to seek the aid and cooperation of another. But it would be far better for such a one could they bring themselves to a vital realization of the omnipotence of their own interior powers.

One may cure another but to be permanently healed one must do it themselves. In this way another may be most valuable as a teacher by bringing one to a clear realization of the power of the forces within, but in every case, in order to have a permanent cure, the work of the self is necessary. Christ's words were almost invariably —Go, and sin no more, or, Thy sins are forgiven thee, thus pointing out the one eternal and never-changing fact that all disease and its consequent suffering is the direct or the indirect result of the violation of law, either consciously or unconsciously, either intentionally, or unintentionally.

Suffering is designed to continue only so long as sin continues, sin not necessarily in the theological, but always in the philosophical sense, though many times in the sense of both. The moment the violation ceases, the moment one comes into perfect harmony with the law, the cause of the suffering ceases, and though there may be residing within the cumulative effects of past violation, the cause is removed, and consequently there can be no more effects in the form of additions, and even the diseased condition that has been induced from past violation will begin to disappear as soon as the right forces are set into activity.

There is nothing that will more quickly and more completely bring one into harmony with the laws under which we live than this vital realization of our oneness with the Infinite Spirit, which is the life of all life. In this there can be no disease, and nothing will more readily remove from the organism the obstructions that have accumulated there, or in other words, the disease that resides there, than this full realization and the complete opening of one's self to this divine inflow. 'I shall put My spirit in you, and ye shall live.'

The moment a person realizes their oneness with the Infinite Spirit they recognize themselves as a spiritual being, and no longer as a mere physical material being. They then no longer make the mistake of regarding themselves as body, subject to ills and diseases, but realize the fact that they are spirit, spirit now as much as they ever will or can be, and that they are the builder and so the master of the body, the house in which they live, and the moment they thus recognize their power as master they cease in any way to allow it the mastery over them.

They no longer fear the elements or any of the forces that they now in ignorance allow to take hold of and affect the body. The moment they realize their own supremacy, instead of fearing them as they did when they were out of harmony with them, they learn to love them. They thus come into harmony with them, or rather, they so order them that they come into harmony with them. He who formerly was the slave has now become the master. The moment we come to love a thing it no longer carries harm for us.

There are almost countless numbers today, weak and suffering in body, who would become strong and healthy if they would only give God an opportunity to do His work. To such I would say, Don't shut out the divine inflow. Do anything else rather than this. Open yourselves to it. Invite it. In the degree that you open yourselves to It, its inflowing tide will course through your bodies a force so vital that the old obstructions that are dominating them today will be driven out before it. 'My words are life to them that find them, and wealth to all their flesh.'

There is a trough through which a stream of muddy water has been flowing for many days. The dirt has gradually collected on its sides and bottom, and it continues to collect as long as the muddy water flows through it. Change this. Open the trough to a swift-flowing stream of clear, crystal water, and in a very little while even the very dirt that has collected on its sides and bottom will be carried away. The trough will be entirely cleansed. It will present in aspect of beauty and no longer an aspect of ugliness. And more, the water that now courses through it will be of value, it will be an agent of refreshment, of health and of strength to those who use it.

Yes, in just the degree that you realize your oneness with the infinite Spirit of Life, and thus actualize your latent possibilities and powers, you will exchange disease for ease, inharmony for harmony, suffering and pain for abounding health and strength. And in the degree that you realize this wholeness, this abounding health and strength in yourself, will you carry it to all with whom you come into contact, for we must remember that health is contagious as well as disease.

I hear it asked, What can be said in a concrete way in regard to the practical application of these truths, so that one can hold themselves in the enjoyment of perfect bodily health, and more, that one may heal themselves of any existing disease? In reply, let it be said that the chief thing that can be done is to point out the great underlying principle, and that each individual must make their own application, one person cannot well make this for another.

First let it be said that the very fact of one's holding the thought of perfect health sets into operation vital forces which will in time be more or less productive of the effect of perfect health. Then speaking more directly in regard to the great principle itself, from its very nature, it is clear that more can be accomplished through the process of realization than through the process of affirmation though for some affirmation may be a help, an aid to realization.

In the degree, however, that you come into a vital realization of your oneness with the Infinite Spirit of Life, whence all life in individual form has come and is continually coming, and in the degree that through this realization you open yourself to its divine inflow do you set into operation forces that will sooner or later bring even the physical body into a state of abounding health and strength. For to realize that this Infinite Spirit of Life can from its very nature admit of no disease, and to realize that this, then, is the life in you by realizing your oneness with it you can so open yourself to its more abundant entrance that the diseased bodily conditions and effects will respond to the influences of its all-perfect power, this either quickly or more tardily, depending entirely upon yourself.

There have been those who have been able to open themselves so fully to this realization that the healing has been instantaneous and permanent. The degree of intensity always eliminates in like degree the element of time. It must, however, be a calm, quiet, and expectant intensity, rather than an intensity that is fearing, disturbed, and non-expectant. Then there are others who have come to this realization by degrees. Many will receive great help, and many will be entirely healed by a practice somewhat after the following nature: With a mind at peace, and with a heart going out in love to all, go into the quiet of your own interior self, holding the thought —I am one with the Infinite Spirit of Life, the life of my life. I then as spirit, a spiritual being, can in my own real nature admit of no disease. I now open my body, in which disease has got a foothold, I open it fully to the inflowing tide of this Infinite Life, and it now, even now, is pouring in and coursing through my body, and the healing process is going on.

Realize this so fully that you begin to feel a quickening and a warm glow imparted by the life forces to the body. Believe the healing process is going on. Believe it, and hold continually to it. Many people greatly desire a certain thing, but expect something else. They have greater faith in the power of evil than in the power of good, and hence remain ill.

If one will give themselves to this meditation, realization, treatment, or whatever term it may seem best to us, at stated times, as often as they may choose, and then continually bold themselves in the same attitude of mind, thus allowing the force to work continually, they will be surprised how rapidly the body will be exchanging conditions of disease and inharmony for health and harmony. There is no particular reason, however, for this surprise, for in this way they are simply allowing the Omnipotent Power to do the work, which will have to do it ultimately in any case.

If there is a local difficulty, and one wants to open this particular portion, in addition to the entire body, to this inflowing life, one can hold this particular portion in thought, for to fix the thought in this way upon any particular portion of the body stimulates or increases the flow of the life forces in that portion. It must always be borne in mind, however, that whatever healing may be thus accomplished, effects will not permanently cease until causes have been removed. In other words, as long as there is the violation of law, so long disease and suffering will result.

This realization that we are considering will have an influence not only where there is a diseased condition of the body, but even where there is not this condition it will give an increased bodily life, vigor, and power.

We have had many cases, in all times and in all countries, of healing through the operation of the interior forces, entirely independent of external agencies. Various have been the methods or rather, various have been the names applied to them, but the great law underlying all is one and the same, and the same today. When the Master sent His followers forth, His injunction to them was to heal the sick and the afflicted, as well as to teach the people. The early Church fathers had the power of healing, in short, it was a part of their work.

And why should we not have the power today, just as they had it then? Are the laws at all different? Identically the same. Why, then? Simply because, with a few rare exceptions here and there, we are unable to get beyond the mere letter of the law into its real vital spirit and power. It is the letter that killeth, it is the spirit that giveth life and power. Every soul who becomes so individualized that they break through the mere letter and enter into the real vital spirit will have the power, as have all who have gone before, and when they do, they will also be the means of imparting it to others, for they will be one who will move and who will speak with authority.

We are rapidly finding today, and we shall find even more and more, as time passes, that practically all disease, with its consequent suffering, has its origin in perverted mental and emotional states and conditions. The mental attitude we take toward anything determines to a greater or less extent its effects upon us. If we fear it, or if we antagonize it, the chances are that it will have detrimental or even disastrous effects upon us. If we come into harmony with it by quietly recognizing and inwardly asserting our superiority over it, in the degree that we are able successfully to do this, in that degree will it carry with it no injury for us.

No disease can enter into or take hold of our bodies unless it find therein something corresponding to itself which makes it possible. And in the same way, no evil or undesirable condition of any kind can come into our lives unless there is already in them that which invites it and so makes it possible for it to come. The sooner we begin to look within ourselves for the cause of whatever comes to us, the better it will be, for so much the sooner will we begin to make conditions within ourselves such that only good may enter.

We, who from our very natures should be masters of all conditions, by virtue of our ignorance are mastered by almost numberless conditions of every description.

Do I fear a draught? There is nothing in the draught—a little purifying current of God's pure air— to cause me trouble, to bring on a cold, perhaps an illness. The draught can affect me only in the degree that I myself make it possible, only in the degree that I allow it to affect me. We must distinguish between causes and mere occasions. The draught is not cause, nor does it carry cause with it. Two persons are sitting in the same draught. The one is injuriously affected by it, the other experiences not even an inconvenience, but they rather enjoy it. The one is a creature of circumstances, they fear the draught, cringe before it, continually think of the harm it is doing them.

In other words, they open every avenue for it to enter and take hold of them, and so it, harmless and beneficent in itself, brings to them exactly what they have empowered it to bring. The other recognizes themselves as the master over and not the creature of circumstances. They are not concerned about the draught. They put themselves into harmony with it, make themselves positive to it, and instead of experiencing any discomfort, they enjoy it, and in addition to its doing them a service by bringing the pure fresh air from without to them, it does them the additional service of hardening them even more to any future conditions of a like nature. But if the draught was cause, it would bring the same results to both. The fact that it does not, shows that it is not a cause, but a condition, and it brings to each, effects which correspond to the conditions it finds within each.

Poor draught! How many thousands, nay millions of times it is made the scapegoat by those who are too ignorant or too unfair to look their own weaknesses square in the face, and who instead of becoming imperial masters remain cringing slaves. Think of it, what it means. A man created in the image of the eternal God, sharer of His life and power, born to have dominion, fearing, shaking, cringing before a little draught of pure life-giving air. But scapegoats are convenient things, even if the only thing they do for us is aid us in our constant efforts at self-delusion.

The best way to disarm a draught of the bad effects it has been accustomed to bring one, is first to bring about a pure and healthy set of conditions within, then, to change one's mental attitude toward it. Recognize the fact that of itself it has no power, it has only the power you invest it with. Thus you will put yourself into harmony with it, and will no longer sit in fear of it. Then sit in a draught a few times and get hardened to it, as everyone, by going at it judiciously, can readily do. 'But suppose one is in delicate health, or especially subject to draughts?' Then be simply a little judicious at first, don't seek the strongest that can be found, especially if you do not as yet in your own mind feel equal to it, for if you do not, it signifies that you still fear it. That supreme regulator of all life, good common sense, must be used here, as elsewhere.

If we are born to have dominion, and that we are is demonstrated by the fact that some have attained to it —and what one has done, soon or late all can do —then it is not necessary that we live under the domination of any physical agent. In the degree that we recognize our own interior powers, then are we rulers and able to dictate; in the degree that we fail to recognize them, we are slaves, and are dictated to. We build whatever we find within us, we attract whatever comes to us, and all in accordance with spiritual law, for all natural law is spiritual law.

The whole of human life is cause and effect, there is no such thing in it as chance, nor is there even in all the wide universe. Are we not satisfied with whatever comes into our lives? The thing to do, then, is not to spend time in railing against the imaginary something we create and call fate, but to look to the within, and change the causes at work there, in order that things of a different nature may come, for there will come exactly what we cause to come.

This is true not only of the physical body, but of all phases and conditions of life. We invite whatever comes, and did we not invite it, either consciously or unconsciously, it could not and it would not come. This may undoubtedly be hard for some to believe, or even to see, at first. But in the degree that one candidly and open-mindedly looks at it, and then studies into the silent, but subtle and, so to speak, omnipotent workings of the thought forces, and as they trace their effects within them and about them, it becomes clearly evident, and easy to understand.

And then whatever does come to one depends for its effects entirely upon their mental attitude toward it. Does this or that occurrence or condition cause you annoyance? Very well, it causes you annoyance, and so disturbs your peace merely because you allow it to. You are born to have absolute control over your own dominion, but if you voluntarily hand over this power, even if for a little while, to some one or to some thing else then you of course become the creature, the one controlled.

To live undisturbed by passing occurrences you must first find your own center. You must then be firm in your own center, and so rule the world from within. He who does not himself condition circumstances allows the process to be reversed, and becomes a conditioned circumstance. Find your center and live in it. Surrender it to no person, to no thing. In the degree that you do this will you find yourself growing stronger and stronger in it. And how can one find their center? By realizing their oneness with the Infinite Power, and by living continually in this realization.

But if you do not rule from your own center, if you invest this or that with the power of bringing you annoyance, or evil, or harm, then take what it brings, but cease your railings against the eternal goodness and beneficence of all things.

> I swear the earth shall surely be complete,
> To him who shall be complete,
> The earth remains jagged and broken
> Only to him who remains jagged and broken.

If the windows of your soul are dirty and streaked, covered with matter foreign to them, then the world as you look out of them will be to you dirty and streaked and out of order. Cease your complainings, however, keep your pessimism, your 'poor, unfortunate me' to yourself, lest you betray the fact that your windows are badly in need of something. But know that your friend, who keeps their windows clean that the Eternal Sun may illuminate all within and make visible all without, know that they live in a different world from yours.

Then, go wash your windows, and instead of longing for some other world you will discover the wonderful beauties of this world, and if you don't find transcendent beauties on every hand here, the chances are that you will never find them anywhere.

> The poem hangs on the berry-bush
> When comes the poet's eye.
> And the whole street is a masquerade
> When Shakespeare passes by.

This same Shakespeare, whose mere passing causes all this commotion, is the one who put into the mouth of one of his creations the words: 'The fault, dear Brutus, is not in our stars, but in ourselves, and we are underlings,' And the great work of his own life is right good evidence that he realized full well the truth of the facts we are considering. And again he gave us a great truth in keeping with what we are considering when he said:

> Our doubts are traitors,
> And make us lose the good we oft might win
> By fearing to attempt.

There is probably no agent that brings us more undesirable conditions than fear. We should live in fear of nothing, nor will we when we come fully to know ourselves. An old French proverb runs:

> Some of your griefs you have cured,
> And the sharpest you still have survived,
> But what torments of pain you endured
> From evils that never arrived.

Fear and lack of faith go hand in hand. The one is born of the other. Tell me how much one is given to fear, and I will tell you how much they lack in faith. Fear is a most expensive guest to entertain, as also is worry; so expensive are they that no one can afford to entertain them. We invite what we fear, just as, by a different attitude of mind, we invite and attract the influences and conditions we desire. The mind dominated by fear opens the door for the entrance of the very things, for the actualization of the very conditions it fears.

'Where are you going?' asked an Eastern pilgrim on meeting the plague one day. 'I am going to Baghdad to kill five thousand people,' was the reply. A few days later the same pilgrim met the plague returning. 'You told me you were going to Baghdad to kill five thousand people,' said he, 'but instead, you killed fifty thousand.' 'No,' said the plague. 'I killed only five thousand, as I told you I would; the others died of fright.'

Fear can paralyze every muscle in the body. Fear affects the flow of the blood, likewise the normal and healthy action of all the life forces. Fear can make the body rigid, motionless, and powerless to move.

Not only do we attract to ourselves the things we fear, but we also aid in attracting to others the conditions we in our own minds hold them in fear of. This we do in proportion to the strength of our own thought, and in the degree that they are sensitively organized and so influenced by our thought, and this although it be unconscious both on their part and on ours.

Children, and especially when very young, are, generally speaking, more sensitive to their surrounding influences than grown people are. Some are veritable little sensitive plates, registering the influences about them, and embodying them as they grow. How careful in their prevailing mental states then should be those who have them in charge, and especially how careful should a mother be during the time she is carrying the child, and when every thought, every mental as well as emotional state has its direct influence upon the life of the unborn child. Let parents be careful how they hold a child, either younger or older, in the thought of fear. This is many times done, unwittingly on their part, through anxiety, and at times through what might well be termed over-care, which is fully as bad as under-care.

I know of a number of cases where a child has been so continually held in the thought of fear lest this or that condition come upon him, that the very things that were feared have been drawn to them, which probably otherwise never would have come at all. Many times there has been no adequate basis for the fear. In case there is a basis, then far wiser it is to take exactly the opposite attitude, so as to neutralize the force at work, and then to hold the child in the thought of wisdom and strength that it may be able to meet the condition and master it, instead of being mastered by it.

But a day or two ago a friend was telling me of an experience of his own life in this connection. At a period when he was having terrific struggle with a certain habit, he was so continually held in the thought of fear by his mother and the young lady to whom he was engaged, the engagement to be consummated at the end of a certain period, the time depending on his proving his mastery, that he, very sensitively organized, continually felt the depressing and weakening effects of their negative thoughts. He could always tell exactly how they felt toward him, he was continually influenced and weakened by their fear, by their questionings, by their suspicions, all of which had the effect of lessening the sense of his own power, all of which had an endeavor-paralyzing influence upon him. And so instead of their begetting courage and strength in him, they brought him to a still greater realization of his own weakness and the almost worthless use of struggle.

Here were two who loved him dearly, and who would have done anything and everything to help him gain the mastery, but who, ignorant of the silent, subtle, ever-working and all-telling power of the thought forces, instead of imparting to him courage, instead of adding to his strength, disarmed him of this, and then added an additional weakness from without. In this way the battle for him was made harder in a three-fold degree.

Fear and worry and all kindred mental states are too expensive for any person, man, woman, or child, to entertain or indulge in. Fear paralyses healthy action, worry corrodes and pulls down the organism, and will finally tear it to pieces. Nothing is to be gained by it, but everything to be lost. Long-continued grief at any loss will do the same. Each brings its own peculiar type of ailment. An inordinate love of gain, a close-fisted, hoarding disposition will have kindred effects. Anger, jealousy, malice, continual fault-finding, lust, has each its own peculiar corroding, weakening, tearing-down effects.

We shall find that not only are happiness and prosperity concomitants of righteousness, living in harmony with the higher laws, but bodily health as well. The great Hebrew seer enunciated a wonderful chemistry of life when he said, 'As righteousness tendeth to life, so he that pursueth evil, pursueth it to his own death.' On the other hand, 'In the way of righteousness is life, and in the pathway thereof there is no death.' The time will come when it will be seen that this means far more than most people dare even to think as yet. 'It rests with man to say whether his soul shall be housed in a stately mansion of ever-growing splendour and beauty, or in a hovel of his own building —a hovel at last ruined and abandoned to decay.'

The bodies of almost untold numbers, living their one-sided unbalanced lives, are every year, through these influences, weakening and falling by the wayside long before their time. Poor, poor houses! Intended to be beautiful temples, brought to desolation by their ignorant, reckless, deluded tenants. Poor houses!

A close observer, a careful student of the power of the thought forces, will soon be able to read in the voice, in the movements the features, the effects registered by the prevailing mental states and conditions. Or, if they are told the prevailing mental states and conditions, they can describe the voice, the movements, the features, as well as describe, in a general way, the peculiar physical ailments their possessor is heir to.

We are told by good authority that a study of the human body, its structure, and the length of time it takes to come to maturity, in comparison with the time it takes the bodies of various animals and their corresponding longevity, reveals the fact that its natural age should be nearer a hundred and twenty years than what we commonly find it today. But think of the multitudes all about us whose bodies are aging, weakening, breaking, so that they have to abandon them long before they reach what ought to be a long period of strong, vigorous middle life. Then, the natural length of life being thus shortened, it comes to be what we might term a race belief that this shortened period is the natural period.

And as a consequence many, when they approach a certain age, seeing that as a rule people at this period of life begin to show signs of age, to break and go downhill, as we say, they, thinking it a matter of course and that it must be the same with them, by taking this attitude of mind many times bring upon themselves these very conditions long before it is necessary. Subtle and powerful are the influences of the mind in the building and rebuilding of the body. As we understand them better it may become the custom for people to look forward with pleasure to the teens of their second century.

There comes to mind at this moment a friend, a lady well on to eighty years of age. An old lady, some, most people in fact, would call her, especially those who measure age by the number of the seasons that have come and gone since one's birth. But to call our friend old would be to call black white. She is no older than a girl of twenty-five, and indeed younger, I am glad to say, or I am sorry to say, depending upon the point of view, than many a girl of this age. Seeking for the good in all people and in all things, she has found the good everywhere. The brightness of disposition and of voice that is hers today, that attracts all people to her and that makes her so beautifully attractive to all people, has characterized her all through life. It has in turn carried brightness and hope and courage and strength to hundreds and thousands of people through all these years, and will continue to do so, apparently, for many years yet to come.

No fears, no worryings, no hatreds, no jealousies, no sorrowings, no grievings, no sordid graspings after inordinate gain, have found entrance into her realm of thought As a consequence her mind, free from these abnormal states and conditions, has not externalized in her body the various physical ailments that the great majority of people are carrying about with them, thinking in their ignorance, that they are natural, and that it is all in accordance with the 'eternal order of things' that they should have them. Her life has been one of varied experiences, so that all these things would have found ready entrance into the realm of her mind and so into her life were she ignorant enough to allow them entrance.

On the contrary she has been wise enough to recognize the fact that in one kingdom at least she is ruler, the kingdom of her mind, and that it is hers to dictate as to what shall and what shall not enter there. She knows, moreover, that in determining this she is determining all the conditions of her life. It is indeed a pleasure as well as an inspiration to see her as she goes here and there, to see her sunny disposition, her youthful step, to hear her joyous laughter. Indeed and in truth, Shakespeare knew whereof he spoke when he said, It 's the mind that makes the body rich.'

With great pleasure I watched her but recently as she was walking along the street, stopping to have a word and so a part in the lives of a group of children at play by the wayside, hastening her step a little to have a word with a washerwoman carrying her bundle of clothes, stopping for a word with a laboring man returning with dinner-can in hand from his work, returning the recognition from the lady in her car, and so imparting some of her own rich life to all with whom she came into contact.

And as good fortune would have it, while still watching her, an old lady passed her, really old, this one, though at least ten or fifteen years younger, so far as the count by the seasons is concerned. Nevertheless, she was bent in form and apparently stiff in joint muscle. Silent in mood, she wore a countenance of long-faced sadness, which was intensified surely several fold by a black, somber headgear with an immense heavy veil, still more somber-looking if possible. Her entire dress was of this description. By this relic-of-barbarism garb, combined with her own mood and expression, she continually proclaimed to the world two things, her own personal sorrows and woes, which by this very method she kept continually fresh in her mind, and also her lack of faith in the eternal goodness of things, her lack of faith in the love and eternal goodness of the Infinite Father.

Wrapped only in the thoughts of her own ailments, and sorrows, and woes, she received and she gave nothing of joy, nothing of hope, nothing of courage, nothing of value to those whom she passed or with whom she came in contact. But on the contrary she suggested to all and helped to intensify in many those mental states all too prevalent in our common human life. And as she passed our friend one could notice a slight turn of the head which, coupled with the expression in her face, seemed to indicate this as her thought —your dress and your conduct are not wholly in keeping with a lady of your years. Thank God, then, thank God they are not. And may He in His great goodness and love send us an innumerable company of the same rare type; and may they live a thousand years to bless mankind, to impart the life-giving influences of their own royal lives to the numerous ones all about us who stand so much in need of them.

Would you remain always young, and would you carry all the loyousness and buoyancy of youth into your mature years? Then have care concerning but one thing, how you live in your thought world. This will determine all. It was the inspired one, Gautama, the Buddha, who said, 'The mind is everything, what you think you become.' And the same thing had Ruskin in mind when he said, 'Make yourself nests of pleasant thoughts. None of us as yet know, for none of us have been taught in early youth, what fairy palaces we may build of beautiful thought, proof against all adversity.' And would you have in your body all the elasticity, all the strength, all the beauty of your younger years? Then live these in your mind, making no room for unclean thought, and you will externalize them in your body. In the degree that you keep young in thought will you remain young in body. And you will find that your body will in turn aid your mind, for body helps mind just as mind builds body,

You are continually building, and so externalizing in your body, conditions most akin to the thoughts and emotions you entertain. And not only are you so building from within, but you are also continually drawing from without forces of a kindred nature. Your particular kind of thought connects you with a similar order of thought from without. If it is bright, hopeful, cheerful, you connect yourself with a current of thought of this nature. If it is sad, fearing, despondent, then this is the order of thought you connect yourself with.

If the latter is the order of your thought, then perhaps unconsciously and by degrees you have been connecting yourself with it. You need to go back and pick up again a part of your child nature, with its careless and cheerful type of thought. The minds of the group of children at play are unconsciously concentrated in drawing to their bodies a current of playful thought. Place a child by itself, deprive it of its companions, and soon it will mope and become slow of movement. It is cut off from that peculiar thought current and is literally "out of its element."

'You need to bring again this current of playful thought to you which has gradually been turned off. You are too serious or sad, or absorbed in the serious affairs of life. You can be playful and cheerful without being puerile or silly. You can carry on business all the better for being in the playful mood when your mind is off your business. There is nothing but ill resulting from the permanent mood of sadness and seriousness — the mood which by many so long maintained makes it actually difficult for them to smile at all.

'At eighteen or twenty you commenced growing out of the more playful tendency of early youth. You took hold of the more serious side of life. You went into some business. You became more or less involved in its cares, perplexities and responsibilities. Or, as man, you entered on some phase of life involving care or trouble. Or you became absorbed in some game of business which, as you followed it, left no time for play. Then as you associated with older people you absorbed their old ideas, their mechanical methods of thinking, their acceptance of errors without question or thought of question.

In all this you opened your mind to a heavy, care-laden current of thought. Into this you glided unconsciously. That thought is materialized in your blood and flesh. The seen of your body is a deposit or crystallization of the unseen element ever "lowing to your body from your mind. Years pass on and you find that your movements are stiff and cumbrous, that you can with difficulty climb a tree, as at fourteen. Your mind has all this time been sending to your body these heavy, inelastic elements, making your body what now it is....

'Your change for the better must be gradual, and can only be accomplished by bringing the thought current of an all-round symmetrical strength to bear on it, by demanding of the Supreme Power to be led in the best way, by diverting your mind from the many unhealthy thoughts which habitually have been flowing into it without your knowing it, to healthier ones....

'Like the beast, the bodies of those of our race have in the past weakened and decayed. This will not always be. Increase of spiritual knowledge will show the cause of such decay, and will show, also, how to take advantage of a Law of Force to build us up, renew ever the body and give it greater and greater strength, instead of blindly using that Law of Force, as has been done in the past, to weaken our bodies and finally destroy them.'

Full, rich and abounding health is the normal and the natural condition of life. Anything else is an abnormal condition, and abnormal conditions as a rule come through perversions. God never created sickness, suffering, and disease, they are man's own creations. They come through his violating the laws under which he lives. So used are we to seeing them that we come gradually, if not to think of them as natural, then to look upon them as a matter of course.

The time will come when the work of the physician will not be to treat and attempt to heal the body, but to heal the mind, which in turn will heal the body. In other words, the true physician will be a teacher, his work will be to keep people well, instead of attempting to make them well after sickness and disease comes or and still beyond this there will come a time when each will be their own physician. In the degree that we live in harmony with the higher laws of our being, and so, in the degree that we become better acquainted with the powers of the mind and spirit, will we give less attention to the body, no less care, but less attention.

The bodies of thousands today would be much better cared for if their owners gave them less thought and attention. As a rule, those who think least of their bodies enjoy the best health. Many are kept in continual ill health by the abnormal thought and attention they give them.

Give the body the nourishment, the exercise, the fresh air, the sunlight it requires, keep it clean, and then think of it as little as possible. In your thoughts and in your conversation never dwell upon the negative side. Don't talk of sickness and disease. By talking of these you do yourself harm and you do harm to those who listen to you. Talk of those things that will make people the better for listening to you. Thus you will infect them with health and strength and not with weakness and disease.

To dwell upon the negative side is always destructive. This is true for the body just as it is true of all other things. The following from one whose thorough training as a physician has been supplemented by extensive study and observations along the lines of the powers of the interior forces, are of special significance and value in this connection:

'We can never gain health by contemplating disease, any more than we can reach perfection by dwelling upon imperfection, or harmony through discord. We should keep a high ideal of health and harmony constantly before the mind....

'Never affirm or repeat about your health what you do not wish to be true. Do not dwell upon your ailments, nor study your symptoms. Never allow yourself to be convinced that you are not complete master of yourself. Stoutly affirm your superiority over bodily ills, and do not acknowledge yourself the slave of any inferior power..... I would teach children early to build a strong barrier between themselves and disease by healthy habits of thought, high thinking, and purity of life. I would teach them to expel all thoughts of death, all images of disease, all discordant emotions, like hatred, malice, revenge, envy, and sensuality, as they would banish a temptation to do evil.

I would teach them that bad food, bad drink, or bad air makes bad blood, that bad blood makes bad tissue, and bad flesh bad morals. I would teach them that healthy thoughts are as essential to healthy bodies as pure thoughts to a clean life. I would teach them to cultivate a strong will power, and to brace themselves against life's enemies in every possible way. I would teach the sick to have hope, confidence cheer. Our thoughts and imaginations are the only real limits to our possibilities. No man's success or health will ever reach beyond his own confidence, as a rule, we erect our own barriers.

'Like produces like the universe through. Hatred, envy, malice jealousy, and revenge all have children. Every bad thought breeds others, and each of these goes on and on, ever reproducing itself, until our world is peopled with their offspring. The true physician and parent of the future will not mediate the body with drugs so much as the mind with principles. The coming mother will teach her child to assuage the fever of anger, hatred, malice, with the great panacea of the world, Love. The coming physician will teach the people to cultivate cheerfulness, goodwill, and noble deeds for a health tonic as well as a heart tonic, and that a merry heart doeth good like a medicine.'

The health of your body, like the health and strength of your mind, depends upon what you relate yourself with. This Infinite spirit of Life, this Source of all Life, can from its very nature, we have found, admit of no weakness, no disease. Come then into the full, conscious, vital realization of your oneness with this Infinite Life, open yourself to its more abundant entrance, and full and ever-renewing bodily health and strength will be yours.

> And good may ever conquer ill,
> Health walk where pain has trod,
> As a man thinketh, so is he,

Rise, then, and think with God.

The whole matter may then be summed up in one sentence, 'God is well and so are you.' You must awaken to the knowledge of your real being. When this awakening comes, you will have, and you will see that you have, the power to determine what conditions are externalized in your body. You must recognize, you must realize yourself as one with Infinite Spirit. God's will is then your will; your will is God's will, and with God all things are possible.' When we are able to do away with all sense of separateness by living continually in the realization of this oneness, not only will our bodily ills and weaknesses vanish, but all limitations along all lines.

Then delight thyself in the Lord, and He shall give thee the desires of thine heart. Then will you feel like crying all the day long, 'The lines are fallen unto me in pleasant places, yea, I have a goodly heritage.' Drop out of mind your belief in good things and good events coming to you in the future. Come now into the real life, and coming, appropriate and actualize them now. Remember that only the best is good enough for one with a heritage so royal as yours.

> We buy ashes for bread,
> We buy diluted wine,
> Give me the true –
> Whose ample leaves and tendrils curled
> Among the silver bills of heaven,
> Draw everlasting dew.

The Secret, Power And Effects Of Love

This is the Spirit of Infinite Love. The moment we recognize ourselves as one with it we become so filled with love that we see only the good in all. And when we realize that we are all one with this Infinite Spirit, then we realize that in a sense we are all one with each other. When we come into a recognition of this fact, we can then do no harm to any one, to any thing. We find that we are all members of the one great body, and that no portion of the body can be harmed without all the other portions suffering thereby.

When we fully realize the great fact of the oneness of all life, that all are partakers from this one Infinite Source, and so that the same life is the life in each individual, then prejudices go and hatreds cease. Love grows and reigns supreme. Then, wherever we go, whenever we come in contact with the fellow man, we are able to recognize the God within. We thus look only for the good, and we find it. It always pays.

There is a deep scientific fact underlying the great truth, 'He that takes the sword shall perish by the sword.' The moment we come into a realization of the subtle powers of the thought forces, we can quickly see that the moment we entertain any thoughts of hatred toward another, they get the effects of these diabolical forces that go out from us, and have the same thoughts of hatred aroused in them, which in turn return to the sender. Then when we understand the effects of the passion, hatred or anger, even upon the physical body, we can see how detrimental, how expensive this is. The same is true in regard to all kindred thoughts or passions, envy, criticism, jealousy, scorn. In the ultimate we shall find that in entertaining feelings of this nature toward another we always suffer far more than the one toward whom we entertain them.

And then when we fully realize the fact that selfishness is at the root of all error, sin, and crime, and that ignorance is the basis of all selfishness, with what charity we come to look upon the acts of all! It is the ignorant man who seeks his own ends at the expense of the greater whole. It is the ignorant man, therefore, who is the selfish man. The truly wise man is never selfish. He is a seer, and recognizes the fact that he, a single member of the one great body, is benefited in just the degree that the entire body is benefited, and so he seeks nothing for himself that he would not equally seek for all mankind.

It selfishness is at the bottom of all error, sin, and crime, and ignorance is the basis of all selfishness, then when we see a manifestation of either of these qualities, if we are true to the highest within us, we will look for and will seek to call forth the good in each individual with whom we come in contact. When God speaks to God, then God responds, and shows forth as God. But when devil speaks to devil, then devil responds, and the devil is always to pay.

I sometimes hear a person say, 'I don't see any good in him.' No? Then you are no seer. Look deeper and you will find the very God in every human soul. But remember it takes a God to recognize a God. Christ always spoke to the highest, the truest, and the best in men. He knew and He recognized the God in each because He had first realized it in Himself. He ate with publicans and sinners. Abominable, the Scribes and Pharisees said. They were so wrapped up in their own conceits, their own self-centeredness, hence their own ignorance, that they had never found the God in themselves, and so they never dreamed that it was the real life of even publicans and sinners.

In the degree that we hold a person in the thought of evil or of error do we suggest evil and error to them. In the degree that they are sensitively organized, or not well individualized, and so, subject to the suggestions of the thought forces from others, will they be influenced, and so in this way we may be sharers in the very evil-doing in which we hold another in thought. In the same way when we hold a person in the thought of the right, the good, and the true, righteousness, goodness, and truth are suggested to them, and thus we have a most beneficent influence on their life and conduct. If our hearts go out in love to all with whom we come in contact, we inspire love, and the same ennobling and warming influences of love always return to us from those in whom we inspire them. There is a deep scientific principle underlying the precept: If you would have all the world love you, you must first love all the world.

In the degree that we love will we be loved. Thoughts are forces. Each creates of its kind. Each comes back laden with the effect that corresponds to itself and of which it is the cause.

> Then let your secret thoughts be fair –
> They have a vital part, and share
> In shaping words and molding fate,
> God's system is so intricate.

I know of no better practice than that of a friend who continually holds himself in an attitude of mind that he continually sends out his love in the form of the thought, 'Dear everybody, I love you.' And when we realize the fact that a thought invariably produces its effect before it returns, or before it ceases, we can see how he is continually breathing out a blessing not only upon all with whom he comes in contact, but upon all the world. These same thoughts of love, moreover, tokened in various ways, are continually coming to him from all quarters.

Even animals feel the effects of these forces. Some animals are much more sensitively organized than many people are, and consequently they get the effects of our thoughts, our mental states, and emotions much more readily than many people do. Therefore whenever we meet an animal we can do it good by sending out to it these thoughts of love. It will feel the effects whether we simply entertain or whether we voice them. And it is often interesting to note how quickly it responds, and how readily it gives evidence of its appreciation of this love and consideration on our part.

What a privilege and how enjoyable it would be to live and walk in a world where we meet only Gods. In such a world you can live. In such a world I can live. For in the degree that we come into this higher realization do we see only the God in each human soul, and when we are thus able to see Him in every one we meet, we then live in such a world. And when we thus recognize the God in everyone, we by this recognition help to call it forth ever more and more. What a privilege, this privilege of yours, this privilege of mine!

That hypocritical judging of another is something then with which we can have nothing to do; for we have the power of looking beyond the evolving, changing, error-making self, and seeing the real, the changeless, the eternal self which by and by will show forth in the full beauty of holiness. We are then large enough also to realize the fact that when we condemn another, by that very act we condemn ourselves.

This realization so fills us with love that we continually overflow it, and all with whom we come in contact feel its warming and life-giving power. These in turn send back the same feelings of love to us, and so we continually attract love from all quarters. Tell me how much one loves and I will tell you how much they have seen of God. Tell me how much they love and I will tell you how much they live with God. Tell me how much they love and I will tell you how far into the Kingdom of Heaven —the kingdom of harmony —they have entered, for 'love is the fulfilling of the law.'

And in a sense love is everything. It is the key to life, and its influences are those that move the world. Live only in the thought of love for all and you will draw love to you from all. Live in the thought of malice or hatred, and malice and hatred will come back to you.

> For evil poisons, malice shafts
> Like boomerangs return,
> Inflicting wounds that will not heal
> While rage and anger burn.

Every thought you entertain is a force that goes out, and every thought comes back laden with its kind. This is an immutable law. Every thought you entertain has moreover a direct effect upon your body. Love and its kindred emotions are the normal and the natural, those in accordance with the eternal order of the universe, for God is love. These have a life-giving, health-engendering influence upon your body, besides beautifying your countenance, enriching your voice, and making you ever more attractive in every way. And as it is true that in the degree that you hold thoughts of love for all, you call the same from them in return, and as these have a direct effect upon your mind, and through your mind upon your body, it is as so much life force added to your own from without. You are then continually building this into both your mental and your physical life, and so your life is enriched by its influence.

Hatred and all its kindred emotions are the unnatural, the abnormal, the perversions, and so, out of harmony with the eternal order of the universe. For if love is the fulfilling of the law then these, its opposites, are direct violations of law, and there can never be a violation of law without its attendant pain and suffering in one form or another. There is no escape from this. And what is the result of this particular form of violation? When you allow thoughts of anger, hatred, malice, jealousy, envy, criticism, or scorn to exercise sway, they have a corroding and poisoning effect upon the organism, they pull it down, and if allowed to continue will eventually tear it to pieces by externalizing themselves in the particular forms of disease they give rise to. And then in addition to the destructive influences from your own mind you are continually calling the same influences from other minds, and these come as destructive forces augmenting your own, thus aiding in the tearing down process.

And so love inspires love; hatred breeds hatred. Love and goodwill stimulate and build up the body; hatred and malice corrode and tear it down. Love is a savior of life unto life; hatred is a savior of death unto death.

> There are loyal hearts, there are spirits brave,
> There are souls that are pure and true,
> Then give to the world the best you have,
> And the best will come back to you.
> Give love, and love to your heart will flow,
> A strength in your utmost need,
> Have faith, and a score of hearts will show,
> Their faith in your word and deed.

I hear it said, How in regard to one who bears me hatred, towards whom I have entertained no such thoughts and feelings, and so have not been the cause of them becoming my enemy? This may be true, but the chances are that you will have but few enemies if there is nothing of an antagonistic nature in your own mind and heart. Be sure there is nothing of this nature. But if hatred should come from another without apparent cause on your part, then meet it from first to last with thoughts of love and goodwill. In this way you can, so to speak, so neutralize its effects that it cannot reach you and so cannot harm you. Love is positive, and stronger than hatred. Hatred can always be conquered by love.

On the other hand, if you meet hatred with hatred, you simply intensify it. You add fuel to the flame already kindled, upon which it will feed and grow, and so you increase and intensify the evil conditions. Nothing is to be gained by it, everything is to be lost. By sending love for hatred you will be able so to neutralize it that it will not only have no effect upon you, but will not be able even to reach you. But more than this, you will by this course sooner or later be able literally to transmute the enemy into the friend. Meet hatred with hatred and you degrade yourself. Meet hatred with love and you elevate not only yourself but also the one who bears you hatred.

The Persian sage has said, 'Always meet petulance with gentleness, and perverseness with kindness. A gentle hand can lead even an elephant by a hair. Reply to thine enemy with gentleness. Opposition to peace is sin.' The Buddhist says, 'If a man foolishly does me wrong I will return him the protection of my ungrudging love. The more evil comes from him the more good shall go from me.' 'The wise man avenges injuries by benefits,' says the Chinese. 'Return good for evil, overcome anger by love; hatred never ceases by hatred, but by love,' says the Hindu.

The truly wise man will recognize no one as an enemy. Occasionally we hear the expression, 'Never mind; I'll get even with him.' Will you? And how will you do it? You can do it in one of two ways. You can, as you have in mind, deal with him as he deals, or apparently deals, with you—pay him, as we say, in his own coin. If you do this you will get even with him by sinking yourself to his level, and both of you will suffer by it. Or, you can show yourself the larger, you can send him love for hatred, kindness for ill-treatment, and so get even with him by raising him to the higher level.

But remember that you can never help another without by that very act helping yourself; and if forgetful of self, then in most cases the value to you is greater than the service you render another. If you are ready to treat him as he treats you, then you show clearly that there is in you that which draws the hatred and ill-treatment to you; you deserve what you are getting and should not complain, nor would you complain if you were wise. By following the other course you most effectually accomplish your purpose, you gain a victory for yourself, and at the same time you do a great service for him, of which it is evident he stands greatly in need.

Thus you may become his savior. He in turn may become the savior of other error-making, and consequently care-encumbered men. Many times the struggles are greater than we can ever know. We need more gentleness and sympathy and compassion in our common human life. Then we will neither blame nor condemn. Instead of blaming or condemning we will sympathize, and all the more we will

> Comfort one another,
> For the way is often dreary,
> And the feet are often weary,
> And the heart is very sad.
> There is a heavy burden bearing,
> When it seems that none are caring,
> And we half forget that ever we were glad.
> Comfort one another
> With the hand-clasp close and tender,
> With the sweetness love can render,
> And the looks of friendly eyes.
> Do not wait with grace unspoken,
> While life's daily bread is broken —
> Gentle speech is oft like manna from the skies.

When we come fully to realize the great fact that all evil and error and sin with all their consequent sufferings come through ignorance then wherever we see a manifestation of these in whatever form, if our hearts are right we will have compassion, sympathy and compassion for the one in whom we see them. Compassion will then change itself into love, and love will manifest itself in kindly service. Such is the divine method. And so instead of aiding in trampling and keeping a weaker one down, we will hold them up until they can stand alone and become the master.

But all life-growth is from within out, and one becomes a true master in the degree that the knowledge of the divinity of their own nature dawns upon the inner consciousness and so brings them into a knowledge of the higher laws; and in no way can we so effectually hasten this dawning in the inner consciousness of another, as by showing forth the divinity within ourselves simply by the way we live.

By example and not by precept. By living, not by preaching. By doing, not by professing. By living the life, not by dogmatizing as to how it should be lived. There is no contagion equal to the contagion of life. Whatever we sow, that shall we also reap, and each thing sown produces of its kind. We can kill not only by doing another bodily injury directly, but we can and we do kill by every antagonistic thought. Not only do we thus kill, but while we kill we commit suicide. Many a man has been made sick by having the ill thoughts of a number of people centered upon him; some have been actually killed. Put hatred into the world and we make it a literal hell. Put love into the world and heaven with all its beauties and glories becomes a reality.

Not to love is not to live, or it is to live a living death. The life that goes out in love to all is the life that is full, and rich, and continually expanding in beauty and in power. Such is the life that becomes ever more inclusive, and hence larger in its scope and influence. The larger the man, the more inclusive they are in their love and their friendships. The smaller the man, the more dwarfed and dwindling their natures, the more they pride themselves upon their 'exclusiveness.' Anyone—a fool or an idiot—can be exclusive. It comes easy. It takes and it signifies a large nature to be universal, to be inclusive.

Only the man of a small, personal, self-centred, self-seeking nature is exclusive. The man of a large, royal, unself-centered nature never is. The small nature is the one that continually strives for effect. The larger nature never does. The one goes here and there in order to gain recognition, in order to attach themselves to the world. The other stays at home and draws the world to them. The one loves merely for themselves. The other loves all the world; but in their larger love for all the world they finds themselves included.

Verily, then, the more one loves the nearer one approaches to God, for God is the Spirit of Infinite Love. And when we come into the realization of our oneness with this Infinite Spirit, then divine love so fills us that, enriching and enrapturing our own lives, from them it flows out to enrich the life of all the world.

In coming into the realization of our oneness with the Infinite Life, we are brought at once into right relations with our fellow man. We are brought into harmony with the great law, that we find our own lives in losing them in the service of others. We are brought to a knowledge of the fact that all life is one, and that we are all parts of the one great whole. We then realize that we cannot serve another without at the same time serving ourselves.

We also realize that we cannot do harm to another without by that very act doing harm to ourselves. We realize that the man who lives to themselves alone lives a little, dwarfed, and stunted life, because they have no part in this larger life of humanity. But the one who in service loses their own life in this larger life, has their own life increased and enriched a thousand or a million fold, and every joy, every happiness, everything of value coming to each member of this greater whole comes as such to them, for they have a part in the life of each and all.

And here let a word be said in regard to true service. Peter and John were one day going up to the temple, and as they were entering the gate they were met by a poor cripple who asked them for alms. Instead of giving him something to supply the day's needs and then leaving him in the same dependent condition for the morrow and the morrow, Peter did him a real service, and a real service for all mankind by saying, Silver and gold have I none, but such as I have I give unto thee. And then he made him whole. He thus brought him into the condition where he could help himself. In other words the greatest service we can do for another is to help them to help themselves. To help them directly might be weakening, though not necessarily. It depends entirely upon circumstances. But to help one to help themselves is never weakening, but always encouraging and strengthening, because it leads them to a larger and stronger life.

There is no better way to help one to help themselves than to bring them to a knowledge of themselves. There is no better way to bring one to a knowledge of themselves than to lead them to a knowledge of the powers that are lying dormant within their own soul. There is nothing that will enable them to come more readily or more completely into an awakened knowledge of the powers that are lying dormant within their own soul, than to bring them into the conscious, vital realization of their oneness with the Infinite Life and Power, so that they may open themselves to it in order that it may work and manifest through them.

We shall find that these same great truths lie at the very bottom of the solution of our social situation; and we shall also find that we shall never have a full and permanent solution of it until they are fully recognized and built upon.

Wisdom And Interior Illumination

This is the Spirit of Infinite Wisdom, and in the degree that we open ourselves to it does the highest wisdom manifest itself to and through us. We can in this way go to the very heart of the universe itself and find the mysteries hidden to the majority of mankind, hidden to them, though not hidden of themselves.

In order for the highest wisdom and insight we must have absolute confidence in the Divine guiding us, but not through the channel of someone else. And why should we go to another for knowledge and wisdom? With God is no respect of persons. Why should we seek these things second hand? Why should we thus stultify our own innate powers? Why should we not go direct to the Infinite Source itself? 'If any man lack wisdom let him ask of God.' 'Before they call I will answer, and while they are yet speaking, I will hear.'

When we thus go directly to the Infinite Source itself we are no longer slaves to personalities, institutions, or books. We should always keep ourselves open to suggestions of truth from these agencies. We should always regard them as agencies, however, and never as sources. We should never recognize them as masters, but simply as teachers. With Browning, we must recognize the great fact that

> Truth is within ourselves, it takes no rise
> From outward things, whate'er you may believe.
> There is an inmost center in us all.
> Where truth abides in fullness.

There is no more important injunction in all the world, nor one with a deeper interior meaning, than 'To thine own self be true.' In other words, be true to your own soul, for it is through your own soul that the voice of God speaks to you. This is the interior guide. This is the light that lighteth every man that cometh into the world. This is conscience. This is intuition. This is the voice of the higher self, the voice of the soul, the voice of God. 'Thou shalt voice behind thee, saying: This is the way, walk ye in it.'

When Elijah was on the mountain it was after the various physical commotions and manifestations that he heard the 'still, small voice,' the voice of his own soul, through which the Infinite God was speaking. If we will but follow this voice of intuition, it will speak ever more clearly and more plainly, until by and by it will be absolute and unerring in its guidance. The great trouble with us is that we do not listen to and do not follow this voice within our own souls, and so we become as a house divided against itself.

We are pulled this way and that, and we are never certain of anything. I have a friend who listens so carefully to this inner voice, who, in other words, always acts so quickly and so fully in accordance with his intuitions, and whose life as a consequence is so absolutely guided by them, that he always does the right thing at the right time and in the right way. He always knows when to act and how to act, and he is never in the condition of a house divided against itself.

But someone says, 'May it not be dangerous for us to act always upon our intuitions? Suppose we should have an intuition to do harm to someone?' We need not be afraid of this, however, for the voice of the soul, this voice of God speaking through the soul, will never direct one to do harm to another, nor to do anything that is not in accordance with the highest standards of right, and truth, and justice. And if you at any time have a prompting of this kind know that it is not the voice of intuition, it is some characteristic of your lower self that is prompting you.

Reason is not to be set aside, but it is to be continually illumined by this higher spiritual perception, and in the degree that it is thus illumined will it become an agent of light and power. When one becomes thoroughly individualized they enter into the realm of all knowledge and wisdom, and to be individualized is to recognize no power outside of the Infinite Power that is at the back of all.

When one recognizes this great fact and opens themselves to this Spirit of Infinite Wisdom, they then enter upon the road to the true education, and mysteries that before were closed now reveal themselves to them This must indeed be the foundation of all true education, this evolving from within, this evolving of what has been involved by the Infinite Power

All things that it is valuable for us to know will come to us if we will but open ourselves to the voice of this infinite Spirit. It is thus that we become seers and have the power of seeing into the very heart of things. There are no new stars, there are no new laws or forces, but we can so open ourselves to this Spirit of Infinite Wisdom that we can discover and recognize those that have not been known before; and in this way they become new to us. When in this way we come into a knowledge of truth we no longer need facts that are continually changing. We can then enter into the quiet of our own interior selves.

We can open the window and look out, and thus gather the facts as we choose. This is true wisdom. 'Wisdom is the knowledge of God.' Wisdom comes by intuition. It far transcends knowledge. Great knowledge, knowledge of many things, may be had by virtue simply of a very retentive memory. It comes by tuition. But wisdom far transcends knowledge in that knowledge is a mere incident of this deeper wisdom.

He who would enter into the realm of wisdom must first divest himself of all intellectual pride. He must become as a little child. Prejudices, preconceived opinions and beliefs always stand in the way of true wisdom. Conceited opinions are always suicidal in their influences. They bar the door to the entrance of truth. All about us we see men in the religious world, in the world of science, in the political, in the social world, who through intellectual pride are so wrapped in their own conceits and prejudices that larger and later revelations of truth can find no entrance to them; and instead of growing and expanding, they are becoming dwarfed and stunted, and still more incapable of receiving truth. Instead of actively aiding in the progress of the world, they are as so many dead sticks in the way that would retard the wheels of progress. This, however, they can never do. Such always in time get bruised, broken, and left behind, while God's triumphal car of truth moves steadily onward.

When the steam engine was still being experimented with, and before it was perfected sufficiently to come into practical use, a well-known Englishman—well known then in scientific circles— wrote an extended pamphlet proving that it would be impossible for it ever to be used in ocean navigation, that is in a trip involving the crossing of the ocean, because it would be utterly impossible for any vessel to carry with it sufficient coal for the use of its furnace. And the interesting feature of the whole matter was that the very first steam vessel that made the trip from England to America had, among its cargo, a part of the first edition of this carefully prepared pamphlet. There was only the one edition. Many editions might be sold now.

This seems indeed an amusing fact; but far more amusing is the man who voluntarily closes himself to truth because, forsooth, it does not come through conventional, or orthodox, or heretofore accepted channels, or because it may not be in full accord with, or possibly may be opposed to, established usages or beliefs. On the contrary—

> Let there be many windows in your soul,
> That all the glory of the universe
> May beautify it. Not the narrow pane
> Of one poor creed can catch the radiant rays
> That shine from countless sources. Tear away
> The blinds of superstition, let the light
> Pour through fair windows, broad as truth itself
> And high as heaven....
> Tune your ear
> To all the worldless music of the stars
> And to the voice of nature, and your heart
> Shall turn to truth and goodness as the plant

Turns to the sun. A thousand unseen hands
Reach down to help you to their peace-crowned heights,
And all the forces of the firmament
Shall fortify your strength. Be not afraid
To thrust aside half-truths and grasp the whole.

There is a great law in connection with the coming of truth. It is this: Whenever a man shuts himself to the entrance of truth on account of intellectual pride, preconceived opinions, prejudices, or for whatever reason, there is a great law which says that truth in its fullness will come to that one from no source. And on the other hand, when a man opens himself fully to the entrance of truth from whatever source it may come, there is an equally great law which says that truth will flow in to him or to her from all sources, from all quarters. Such becomes the free man, for it is the truth that makes us free. The other remains in bondage, for truth has had no invitation and will not enter where it is not fully and freely welcomed.

And where truth is denied entrance the rich blessings it carries with it cannot take up their abode. On the contrary, when this is the case it sends an envoy carrying with it atrophy, disease, death, physically and spiritually as well as intellectually. And the man who would rob another of his free and unfettered search for truth, who would stand as the interpreter of truth for another, with the intent of remaining in this position, rather than endeavoring to lead him to the place where he can be his own interpreter, is more to be shunned than a thief and a robber. The injury he works is far greater, for he is doing direct and positive injury to the very life of the one he thus holds.

Who has ever appointed any man, whoever they may be, as the keeper, the custodian, the dispenser of God's illimitable truth? Many indeed are moved and so are called to be teachers of truth; but the true teacher will never stand as the interpreter of truth for another. The true teacher is the one whose endeavor is to bring the one they teach to a true knowledge of himself and hence of his or her own interior powers, that they may become their own interpreter. All others are, generally speaking, those animated by purely personal motives, self-aggrandizement, or personal gain. Moreover, he who would claim to have all truth and the only truth, is a bigot, a fool, or a knave.

In the Eastern literature is a fable of a frog. The frog lived in a well, and out of his little well he had never been. One day a frog whose home was in the sea came to his well. Interested in all things, he went in. 'Who are you? Where do you live?' said the frog in the well. 'I am so and so, and my home is in the sea.' 'The sea? What is that? Where is that?' 'It is a very large body of water, and not far away.' 'How big is your sea?' 'Oh, very big.' 'As big as this?' pointing to a little stone lying near. 'Oh, much bigger.' 'As big as this?' pointing to the board upon which they were sitting. 'Oh, much bigger.' 'How much bigger, then?' 'Why, the sea in which I live is bigger than your entire well; it would make millions of wells such as yours.' 'Nonsense, nonsense; you are a deceiver and a falsifier. Get out of my well. Get out of my well. I want nothing to do with any such frogs as you.'

'Ye shall know the truth and the truth shall make you free,' is the promise. Ye shall close yourselves to truth, ye shall live in your own conceits, and your own conceits shall make fools and idiots of you, would be a statement applicable to not a few, and to not a few who pride themselves upon their superior intellectual attainments. Idiocy is arrested mental growth. Closing one's self for whatever reason to truth and hence to growth brings a certain type of idiocy, though it may not be called by this name. And on the other hand, another type is that arrested growth caused by taking all things for granted, without proving them for one's self, merely because they come from a particular person, a particular book, a particular institution. This is caused by one's always looking without instead of being true to the light within, and carefully tending it that it may give an ever-clearer light. With brave and intrepid Walt Whitman, we should all be able to say:

> From this hour I ordain myself loos'd of limits and imaginary lines,
> Going where I list, my own master total and absolute,
> Listening to others, considering well what they say,
> Pausing, searching, receiving, contemplating,
> Gently, but with undeniable will divesting myself of the holds that would hold me.

Great should be the joy that God's boundless truth is open to all, open equally to all, and that it will make each one its dwelling place in proportion as they earnestly desire it and open themselves to it.

And in regard to the wisdom that guides us in our daily life, there is nothing that it is right and well for us to know that may not be known when we recognize the law of its coming, and are able wisely to use it. Let us know that all things are ours as soon as we know how to appropriate them.

> I hold it as a changeless law,
> From which no soul can sway or swerve,
> We have that in us which will draw
> Whate'er we need or most deserve.

If the times come when we know not what course to pursue, when we know not which way to turn, the fault lies in ourselves. If the fault lies in ourselves then the correction of this unnatural condition lies also in ourselves. It is never necessary to come into such a state if we are awake, and remain awake, to the light and the powers within us. The light is ever shining, and the only thing that it is necessary for us diligently to see to is that we permit neither this thing nor that to come between us and the light. 'With Thee is the fountain of life; in Thy light shall we see light.'

Let us hear the words of one of the most highly illumined men I have ever known, and one who as a consequence is never in the dark, when the time comes, as to what to do and how to do it. 'Whenever you are in doubt as to the course you should pursue, after you have turned to every outward means of guidance, let the inward eye see, let the inward ear hear, and allow this simple, natural beautiful process to go on unimpeded by questionings or doubts....

'In all dark hours and times of unwanted perplexity we need to follow one simple direction, found, as all needed directions can be found, in the dear old gospel, which so many read, but alas, so few interpret. "Enter into thine inner chamber and shut the door." Does this mean that we must literally betake ourselves to a private closet with a key in the door? If it did, then the command could never be obeyed in the open air, on land or sea, and the Christ loved the lakes and the forests far better than the cramping rooms of city dwelling houses; still His counsels are so wide-reaching that there is no spot on earth and no conceivable situation in which any of us may be placed where we cannot follow them.

'One of the most intuitive men we ever met had a desk in a city office, where several other gentlemen were doing business constantly and often talking loudly. Entirely undisturbed by the many various sounds about him, this self-centered, faithful man would, in any moment of perplexity, draw the curtains of privacy so completely about him that he would be as fully enclosed in his own psychic aura, and thereby as effectually removed from all distractions as though he were alone in some primeval wood. Taking his difficulty with him into the mystic silence in the form of a direct question, to which he expected a certain answer, he would remain utterly passive until the reply came, and never once through many years' experience did he find himself disappointed or misled.

'Intuitive perceptions of truth are the daily bread to satisfy our daily hunger; they come like the manna in the desert day by day; each day brings adequate supply for that day's need only. They must be followed instantly, for dalliance with them means their obscuration, and the more we dally the more we invite erroneous impressions to cover intuition with a pall of conflicting moral fantasy born of illusions of the terrene will.

'One condition is imposed by universal law, and this we must obey. Put all wishes aside save the one desire to know truth; couple with this one demand, the fully consecrated determination to follow what is distinctly perceived as truth immediately it is revealed. No other affection must be permitted to share the field with this all-absorbing love of truth for its own sake. Obey this one direction, and never forget that expectation and desire are bride and bridegroom and forever inseparable, and you will soon find your hitherto darkened way grow luminous with celestial radiance, for with the heaven within, all heavens without incessantly cooperate.'

This may be termed going into the 'silence.' This it is to perceive and to be guided by the light that lighteth every man that cometh into the world. This it is to listen to and be guided by the voice of your own soul, the voice of your higher self.

The soul is divine and in allowing it to become translucent to the Infinite Spirit it reveals all things to us. As man turns away from the Divine Light do all things become hidden. There is nothing hidden of itself. When the spiritual sense is opened, then it transcends all the limitations of the physical senses and the intellect. And in the degree that we are able to get away from the limitations set by them, and realize that so far as the real life is concerned it is one with the Infinite Life, then we begin to reach the place where its voice will always speak, where it will never fail us, if we follow it, and as a consequence where we shall always have the divine illumination and guidance. To know this and to live in this realization is not to live in heaven hereafter, but to live in heaven here and now, today and every day.

No human soul need be without it. When we turn our face in the right direction it comes as simply and as naturally as the flower blooms and the winds blow. It is not to be bought with money or with price. It is a condition waiting simply to be realized, by rich and by poor, by king and by peasant, by master and by servant the world over. All are equal heirs to it. And so the peasant, if he find it first, lives a life far transcending in beauty and in real power the life of his king. The servant, if he find it first, lives a life surpassing the life of his master.

If you would find the highest, the fullest, and the richest life that not only this world but that any world can know, then do away with the sense of separateness of your life from the life of God. Hold to the thought of your oneness. In the degree that you do this you will find yourself realizing it more and more, and as this life of realization is lived, you will find that no good thing will be withheld, for all things are included in this. Then it will be yours, without fears or forebodings, simply to do today what your hands find to do, and so be ready for tomorrow, when it comes, knowing that tomorrow will bring tomorrow's supplies for the mental, the spiritual, and the physical life. Remember, however, that tomorrow's supplies are not needed until tomorrow comes.

If one is willing to trust themselves fully to the Law, the Law will never fail them. It is the half-hearted trusting to it that brings uncertain, and so, unsatisfactory results. Nothing is firmer and surer than Deity. It will never fail the one who throws themselves wholly upon it. The secret of life then is to live continually in this realization, whatever one may be doing, wherever one may be, by day and by night, both waking and sleeping. It can be lived in while we are sleeping no less than when we are awake. And here shall we consider a few facts in connection with sleep, in connection with receiving instruction and illumination while asleep?

During the process of sleep it is merely the physical body that is at rest and in quiet, the soul life with all its activities goes right on. Sleep is nature's provision for the recuperation of the body, for the rebuilding and hence the replacing of the waste that is continually going on during the waking hours. It is nature's great restorer. If sufficient sleep is not allowed the body, so that the rebuilding may equalize the wasting process, the body is gradually depleted and weakened, and any ailment or malady, when it is in this condition, is able to find a more ready entrance. It is for this reason that those who are subject to it will take a cold, as we term it, more readily when the body is tired or exhausted through loss of sleep than at any other time. The body is in that condition where outside influences can have a more ready effect upon it than when it is in its normal condition. And when they do have an effect they always go to the weaker portions first.

Our bodies are given us to serve far higher purposes than we ordinarily use them for. Especially is this true in the numerous cases where the body is master of its owner. In the degree that we come into the realization of the higher powers of the mind and spirit, in that degree does the body, through their influence upon it, become less gross and heavy, finer in its texture and form. And then, because the mind finds a kingdom of enjoyment in itself, and in all the higher things it becomes related to, excesses in eating and drinking, as well as all others, naturally and of their own accord fall away.

There also falls away the desire for the heavier, grosser, less valuable kinds of food and drink, such as the flesh of animals, alcoholic drinks, and all things of the class that stimulate the body and the passions rather than build the body and the brain into a strong, clean, well-nourished, enduring, and fibrous condition. In the degree that the body thus becomes less gross and heavy, finer in its texture and form, is there less waste, and what there is is more easily replaced, so that it keeps in a more regular and even condition. When this is true, less sleep is actually required. And even the amount that is taken does more for a body of the finer type than it can do for one of the other nature.

As the body in this way grows finer, in other words, as the process of its evolution is thus accelerated, it in turn helps the mind and the soul in the realization of ever higher perceptions, and thus body helps mind just as mind builds body. It was undoubtedly this fact that Browning had in mind when he said:

Let us cry "All good things
Are ours, nor soul helps flesh, more now,
Than flesh helps soul."

Sleep, then, is for the resting and the rebuilding of the body. The soul needs no rest, and while the body is at rest in sleep the soul life is just as active as when the body is in activity.

There are some, having a deep insight into the soul's activities, who say that we travel when we sleep. Some are able to recall and bring over into the conscious, waking life the scenes visited, the information gained, and the events that have transpired.

Most people are not able to do this and so much that might otherwise be gained is lost. They say, however, that it is in our power, in proportion as we understand the laws, to go where we will and to bring over into the conscious, waking life all the experiences thus gained. Be this, however, as it may, it certainly is true that while sleeping we have the power, in a perfectly normal and natural way, to get much of value by way of light, instruction, and growth that the majority of people now miss.

If the soul life, that which relates us to Infinite Spirit, is always active, even while the body is at rest, why may not the mind so direct conditions, as one falls asleep, that while the body is at rest it may continually receive illumination from the soul, and bring what it thus receives over into the conscious, waking life? This, indeed, can be done, and is done by some to great advantage; and many times the highest inspirations from the soul come in this way, as would seem most natural, since at this time all communications from the outer, material world no longer enter. I know those who do much work during sleep, and who get much light along desired lines. By charging the mind on going to sleep as to a particular time for waking, it is possible, as many of us know, to wake on the very minute. Not infrequently we have examples of difficult problems, problems that defied solution during waking hours, being solved during sleep.

A friend, a well-known journalist, had an extended newspaper article clearly and completely worked out for her in this way. She frequently calls this agency to her aid. She was notified by the managing editor one evening to have the article ready in the morning, an article requiring more than ordinary care, and one in which quite a knowledge of facts was required. It was a matter in connection with which she knew scarcely anything, and all her efforts to find information regarding it seemed to be of no avail.

She set to work, but it seemed as if even her own powers defied her. Failure seemed imminent. Almost in desperation she decided to retire, and putting the matter into her mind in such a way that she would be able to receive the greatest amount of aid while asleep, she fell asleep and slept soundly until morning. When she awoke her work of the previous evening was the first thing that came into her mind. She lay quietly for a few minutes, and as she lay there, the article, completely written, seemed to stand before her mind. She ran through it, arose, and without dressing took her pen and transcribed it on to paper, literally acting simply as her own amanuensis.

The mind acting intently along a particular line will continue so to act until some other object of thought carries it along another line. And since in sleep only the body is in quiet while the mind and soul are active, then the mind on being given a certain direction when one drops off to sleep, will take up the line along which it is directed, and can be made, in time, to bring over into consciousness the results of its activities. Some will be able very soon to get results of this kind, for some it will take longer. Quiet and continued effort will increase the faculty.

Then by virtue of the law of the drawing power of mind, since the mind is always active, we are drawing to us even when sleeping influences from the realms kindred to those in which we in our thoughts are living before we fall asleep. In this way we can put ourselves into relation with whatever kinds of influence we choose, and accordingly gain much during the process of sleep. In many ways the interior faculties are more open and receptive while we are in sleep than while we are awake. Hence the necessity of exercising even greater care as to the nature of the thoughts that occupy the mind as we enter into sleep, for there can come to us only what we by our own order of thought attract. We have it entirely in our own hands.

And for the same reason—this greater degree of receptivity during this period—we are able by understanding and using the law to gain much of value more readily in this way than when the physical senses are fully open to the material world about us. Many will find a practice somewhat after the following nature of value: When light or information is desired along any particular line, light or information you feel it is right and wise for you to have, as, for example, light in regard to an uncertain course of action, then as you retire, first bring your mind into the attitude of peace and goodwill for all. You in this way bring yourself into an harmonious condition, and in turn attract to yourself these same peaceful conditions from without.

Then resting in this sense of peace, quietly and calmly send out your earnest desire for the needed light or information; cast out of your mind all fears or forebodings lest it come not, for 'in quietness and in confidence shall be your strength.' Take the expectant attitude of mind, firmly believing and expecting that when you awake the desired results will be with you. Then on awaking, before any thoughts or activities from the outside world come in to absorb the attention, remain for a little while receptive to the intuitions or the impressions that come. When they come, when they manifest themselves clearly, then act upon them without delay. In the degree that you do this, in that degree will the power of doing it ever more effectively grow.

Or, if for unselfish purposes you desire to grow and develop any of your faculties, or to increase the health and strength of your body, take a corresponding attitude of mind, the form of which will readily suggest itself in accordance with your particular needs or desires. In this way you will open yourself to, you will connect yourself with, and you will set into operation within yourself, the particular order of forces that will make for these results.

Don't be afraid to voice your desires. In this way you set into operation vibratory forces which go out and which make their impress felt somewhere, and which, arousing into activity or uniting with other forces, set about to actualize your desires. No good thing shall be withheld from those who live in harmony with the higher laws and forces. There are no desires that shall not be satisfied to the one who knows and who wisely uses the powers with which he is endowed.

Your sleep will be more quiet, and peaceful, and refreshing, and so your power increased mentally, physically, and spiritually, simply by sending out as you fall asleep, thoughts of love and goodwill, thoughts of peace and harmony for all. In this way you are connecting yourself with all the forces in the universe that make for peace and harmony.

A friend who is known the world over through his work along humane lines, has told me that many times in the middle of the night he is awakened suddenly and there comes to his mind, as a flash of inspiration, a certain plan in connection with his work. And as he lies there quietly and opens himself to it, the methods for its successful carrying out all reveal themselves to him clearly. In this way many plans are entered upon and brought to a successful culmination that otherwise would never be thought of, plans that seem, indeed, marvelous to the world at large.

He is a man with a sensitive organism, his life in thorough harmony with the higher laws, and given wholly and unreservedly to the work to which he has dedicated it. Just how and from what source these inspirations come he does not fully know. Possibly no one does, though each may have their theory. But this we do know, and it is all we need to know now, at least, that to the one who lives in harmony with the higher laws of their being, and who opens themselves to them, they come.

Visions and inspirations of the highest order will come in the degree that we make for them the right conditions. One who has studied deeply the subject in hand has said: 'To receive education spiritually while the body is resting in sleep is a perfectly normal and orderly experience, and would occur definitely and satisfactorily in the lives of all of us, if we paid more attention to internal and consequently less to external states with their supposed but unreal necessities....

Our thoughts make us what we are here and hereafter, and our thoughts are often busier by night than by day, for when we are asleep to the exterior we can be wide awake to the interior world; and the unseen world is a substantial place, the conditions of which are entirely regulated by mental and moral attainments. When we are not deriving information through outward avenues of sensation, we are receiving instruction through interior channels of perception, and when this fact is understood for what it is worth, it will become a universal custom for persons to take to sleep with them the special subject on which they most earnestly desire particular instruction. The Pharaoh type of person dreams, and so do his butler and baker; but the Joseph type, which is that of the truly gifted seer, both dreams and interprets'.

But why had not Pharaoh the power of interpreting his dreams? Why was Joseph the type of the 'truly gifted seer'? Why did he not only dream, but had also the power to interpret both his own dreams and the dreams of others? Simply read the lives of the two. He who runs may read. In all true power it is, after all, living the life that tells. And in proportion as one lives the life do they not only attain to the highest power and joy for themselves, but also become of ever greater service to all the world. They need remain in no hell longer than they themselves choose to; and the moment they choose not to remain longer, not all the powers in the universe can prevent them leaving it. One can rise to any heaven one chooses; and when a person chooses so to rise, all the higher powers of the universe combine to help them heavenward.

When one awakes from sleep and so returns to conscious life, they are in a peculiarly receptive and impressionable state. All relations with the material world have for a time been shut off, the mind is in a freer and more natural state, resembling somewhat a sensitive plate, where impressions can readily leave their traces. This is why many times the highest and truest impressions come to one in the early morning hours, before the activities of the day and then attendant distractions have exerted an influence. This is one reason why many people can do their best work in the early hours of the day.

But this fact is also a most valuable one in connection with the molding of everyday life The mind is at this time as a clean sheet of paper. We can most valuably use this quiet, receptive impressionable period by wisely directing the activities of the mind along the highest and most desirable paths, and thus, so to speak set the pace for the day.

Each morning is a fresh beginning. We are, as it were just beginning life. We have it entirely in our own hands. And when the morning with its fresh beginning comes, all yesterdays should be yesterdays, with which we have nothing to do. Sufficient is it to know that the way we lived our yesterday has determined for us our today. And, again, when the morning with its fresh beginning comes, all tomorrows should be tomorrows, with which we have nothing to do. Sufficient to know that the way we live our today determines our tomorrow.

> Every day is a fresh beginning.
> Every morn is the world made new,
> You who are weary of sorrow and sinning,
> Here is a beautiful hope for you,
> A hope for me and a hope for you.
>
> All the past things are past and over,
> The tasks are done, and the tears are shed.
> Yesterday's errors let yesterday cover.
> Yesterday's wounds, which smarted and bled,
> Are healed with the healing which night has shed.
>
> Let them go, since we cannot relieve them,
> Cannot undo and cannot atone.
> God in His mercy receive, forgive them!
> Only the new days are our own.
> Today is ours, and today alone.
>
> Here are the skies all burnished brightly;
> Here is the spent earth all reborn,
> Here are the tired limbs springing lightly
> To face the sun and to share with the morn
> In the chrism of dew and the cool of dawn.
>
> Every day is a fresh beginning,
> Listen, my soul, to the glad refrain,
> And, spite of old sorrow and older sinning,
> And puzzles forecasted, and possible pain,
> Take heart with the day and begin again.

Simply the first hour of this new day, with all its richness and glory, with all its sublime and eternity-determining possibilities, and each succeeding hour as it comes, but not before it comes. This is the secret of character building. This simple method will bring anyone to the realization of the highest life that can be even conceived of, and there is nothing in this connection that can be conceived of that cannot be realized somehow, somewhen, somewhere.

This brings such a life within the possibilities of all, for there is no one, if really in earnest and if they really desire it, who cannot live to their highest for a single hour. But even though there should be, if they are only earnest in their endeavor then, through the law that like builds like, they will be able to come a little nearer to it the next hour, and still nearer the next, and the next, until sooner or later comes the time when it becomes the natural, and any other would require the effort.

In this way one becomes in love and in league with the highest and best in the universe, and as a consequence, the highest and best in the universe becomes in love and in league with them. They aid them at every turn; they seem literally to move all things their way, because forsooth, they have first moved their way.

The Realization Of Perfect Peace

This is the Spirit of Infinite Peace, and the moment we come into harmony with it there comes to us an inflowing tide of peace, for peace is harmony. A deep interior meaning underlies the great truth, 'To be spiritually minded is life and peace.' To recognize the fact that we are spirit, and to live in this thought, is to be spiritually minded and so to be in harmony and peace. Oh, the thousands of men all about us weary with care, troubled and ill at ease, running hither and thither to find peace, weary in body, soul, and mind; going to other countries, traveling the world over, coming back, and still not finding it. Of course they have not found it and they never will find it in this way, because they are looking for it where it is not. They are looking for it without when they should look within. Peace is to be found only within, and unless one find it there they will never find it at all.

Peace lies not in the external world. It lies within one's own soul. We may travel over many different avenues in pursuit of it, we may seek it through the channels of the bodily appetites and passions, we may seek it through all the channels of the external, we may chase for it hither and thither, but it will always be just beyond our grasp, because we are searching for it where it is not. In the degree, however, that we order the bodily appetites and passions in accordance with the promptings of the soul within will the higher forms of happiness and peace enter our lives; but in the degree that we fail in doing this will disease, suffering, and discontent enter in.

To be at one with God is to be at peace. The child simplicity is the greatest agency in bringing this full and complete realization, the child simplicity that recognizes its true relations with the Father's life. There are people I know who have come into such a conscious realization of their oneness with this Infinite Life, this Spirit of Infinite Peace, that their lives are fairly bubbling over with joy.

I have particularly in mind at this moment a comparatively young man who was an invalid for several years, his health completely broken with nervous exhaustion, who thought there was nothing in life worth living for, to whom everything and everybody presented a gloomy aspect, and he in turn presented a gloomy aspect to all with whom he came in contact. Not long ago he came into such a vital realization of his oneness with this Infinite Power, he opened himself so completely to its divine inflow, that today he is in perfect health, and frequently as

I meet him now he cannot resist the impulse to cry out, 'Oh, it is a joy to be alive.'

I know an officer in our police force who has told me that many times when off duty and on his way home in the evening, there comes to him such a vivid and vital realization of his oneness with this Infinite Power, and this Spirit of Infinite Peace so takes hold of and so fills him that it seems as if his feet could scarcely keep to the pavement, so buoyant and so exhilarated does he become by reason of this inflowing tide.

He who comes into this higher realization never has any fear, for he has always with him a sense of protection, and the very realization of this makes his protection complete. Of him it is true, 'No weapon that is formed against thee shall prosper'; 'There shall no ill come nigh thy dwelling'; Thou shall be in league with the stones of the field, and the beasts of the field shall be at peace with thee.'

These are the men who seem to live charmed lives. The moment we fear anything we open the door for the entrance of the actualization of the very thing we fear. An animal will never harm a person who is absolutely fearless in regard to it The instant one fears they open themselves to danger; and some animals, the dog for example, can instantly detect the element of fear, and this gives them the courage to do harm.

In the degree that we come into a full realization of our oneness with this Infinite Power do we become calm and quiet, undisturbed by the little occurrences that before so vex and annoy us. We are no longer disappointed in people, for we always read them aright. We have the power of penetrating into their very souls and seeing the underlying motives that are at work there.

A gentleman approached a friend the other day, and with great show of cordiality grasped him by the hand and said, 'Why, Mr. —, I am so glad to see you.' Quick as a flash my friend read him, and looking him steadily in the eye, replied, 'No, you are mistaken, you are not glad to see me; but you are very much disconcerted, so much so that you are now blushing in evidence of it.' The gentleman replied, 'Well, you know in this day and age of conventionality and form we have to put on the show and sometimes make believe what we do not really feel.' My friend once more looked him in the face and said, 'Again you are mistaken. Let me give you one little word of advice: You will always fare better and will think far more of yourself, always to recognize and to tell the truth rather than to give yourself to any semblance of it.'

As soon as we are able to read people aright we will then cease to be disappointed in them, we will cease to place them on pedestals, for this can never be done without some attendant disappointment. The fall will necessarily come, sooner or later, and moreover, we are thus many times unfair to our friends. When we come into harmony with this Spirit of Peace, evil reports and apparent bad treatment, either at the hands of friends or of enemies, will no longer disturb us. When we are conscious of the fact that in our life and our work we are true to that eternal principle of right, of truth, of justice that runs through all the universe, that unites and governs all, that always eventually prevails, then nothing of this kind can come nigh us, and come what may we will always be tranquil and undisturbed.

The things that cause sorrow, and pain, and bereavement will not be able to take the hold of us they now take, for true wisdom will enable us to see the proper place and know the right relations of all things. The loss of friends by the transition we call death will not cause sorrow to the soul that has come into this higher realization, for they know that there is no such thing as death, for each one is not only a partaker, but an eternal partaker, of this Infinite Life. He knows that the mere falling away of the physical body by no means affects the real soul life. With a tranquil spirit born of a higher faith they can realize for themselves, and to those less strong can say:

Loving friends! be wise and dry
Straightway every weeping eye;
What you left upon the bier
Is not worth a single tear,
'Tis a simple sea-shell, one
Out of which the pearl has gone.
The shell was nothing, leave it there.
The pearl—the soul—was all, is here.

And so far as the element of separation is concerned, he realizes that to spirit there are no bounds, and that spiritual communion, whether between two persons in the body, or two persons, one in the body and one out of the body, is within the reach of all. In the degree that the higher spiritual life is realized can there be this higher spiritual communion.

The things that we open ourselves to always come to us. People in the olden times expected to see angels and they saw them; but there is no more reason why they should have seen them than that we should see them now; no more reason why they should come and dwell with them than that they should come and dwell with us, for the great laws governing all things are the same today as they were then. If angels come not to minister unto us it is because we do not invite them, it is because we keep the door closed through which they otherwise might enter.

In the degree that we are filled with this Spirit of Peace by thus opening ourselves to its inflow does it pour through us, so that we carry it with us wherever we go. In the degree that we thus open ourselves do we become magnets to attract peace from all sources; and in the degree that we attract and embody it in ourselves are we able to give it forth to others. We can in this way become such perfect embodiments of peace that wherever we go we are continually shedding benedictions.

But a day or two ago I saw a woman grasp the hand of a man (his face showed the indwelling God), saying, 'Oh, it does me so much good to see you. I have been in anxiety and almost in despair during the past few hours, but the very sight of you has rolled the burden entirely away.' There are people all around us who are continually giving out blessings and comfort, persons whose mere presence seems to change sorrow into joy, fear into courage, despair into hope, weakness into power.

It is the one who has come into the realization of their own true self who carries this power with them and who radiates it wherever they go, the one who, as we say, has found their center. And in all the great universe there is but one center, the Infinite Power that is working in and through all. The one who then has found their center is the one who has come into the realization of their oneness with this Infinite Power, the one who recognizes themselves as a spiritual being, for God is spirit.

Such is the man of power. Centered in the Infinite, they have thereby, so to speak, connected themselves with, have attached their belts to, the great power-house of the universe. They are constantly drawing power to themselves from all sources. For, thus centered, knowing themselves, conscious of their own power, the thoughts that go from their mind are thoughts of strength, and by virtue of the law that like attracts like, they by their thoughts are continually attracting to themselves from all quarters the aid of all whose thoughts are thoughts of strength, and in this way they are linking themselves with this order of thought in the universe.

And so to them that hath, to them shall be given. This is simply the working of a natural law. Their strong, positive, and hence constructive thought is continually working success for them along all lines, and continually bringing to them help from all directions. The things that they see, that they create in the ideal, are through the agency of this strong constructive thought continually clothing themselves, taking form, manifesting themselves in the material. Silent, unseen forces are at work which will sooner or later be made manifest in the visible.

Fear and all thoughts of failure never suggest themselves to such a man; or if they do, they are immediately sent out of their mind, and so they are not influenced by this order of thought from without. They does not attract it to them. They are in another current of thought. Consequently the weakening, failure-bringing thoughts of the fearing, the vacillating, the pessimistic about them, have no influence upon them.

The one who is of the negative, fearing kind not only has their energies and physical agents weakened, or even paralyzed through the influence of this kind of thought that is born within them, but also in this way connect themselves with this order of thought in the world about them. And in the degree that they do this do they become a victim to the weak, fearing, negative minds all around them. Instead of growing in power, they increase in weakness. They are in the same order of thought with those of whom it is true—and even that which they have shall be taken away from them. This again is simply the working of a natural law, just as is its opposite. Fearing lest I lose even what I have I hide it away in a napkin. Very well. I must then pay for the price of my 'fearing lest I lose.'

Thoughts of strength both build strength from within and attract it from without. Thoughts of weakness actualize weakness from within and attract it from without. Courage begets strength, fear begets weakness. And so courage begets success, fear begets failure. It is the man of faith, and hence of courage who is the master of circumstances, and who makes his or her power felt in the world. It is the man who lacks faith and who as a consequence is weakened and crippled by fears and forebodings, who is the creature of all passing occurrences.

Within each one lies the cause of whatever comes to them. Each has it in their own hands to determine what comes. Everything in the visible, material world has its origin in the unseen, the spiritual, the thought world. This is the world of cause, the former is the world of effect. The nature of the effect is always in accordance with the nature of the cause. What one lives in their invisible, thought world, is continually actualizing in their visible, material world. If he would have any conditions different in the latter they must make the necessary change in the former. A clear realization of this great fact would bring success to thousands of men who all about us are now in the depths of despair. It would bring health, abounding health and strength to thousands now diseased and suffering. It would bring peace and joy to thousands now unhappy and ill at ease.

And oh, the thousands all about us who are continually living in the slavery of fear. The spirits within that should be strong and powerful, are rendered weak and impotent. Their energies are crippled, their efforts are paralyzed. 'Fear is everywhere —fear of want, fear of starvation, fear of public opinion, fear of private opinion, fear that what we own today may not be ours tomorrow, fear of sickness, fear of death. Fear has become with millions a fixed habit. The thought is everywhere. The thought is thrown upon us from every direction.... To live in continual dread, continual cringing, continual fear of anything, be it loss of love, loss of money, loss of position or situation, is to take the readiest means to lose what we fear we shall.'

By fear nothing is to be gained, but on the contrary, everything is to be lost. 'I know this is true,' says one, 'but I am given to fear; it's natural to me and I can't help it.' Can't help it! In saying this you indicate one great reason of your fear by showing that you do not even know yourself as yet. You must know yourself in order to know your powers, and not until you know them can you use them wisely and fully. Don't say you can't help it. If you think you can't the chances are that you can't.

If you think you can, and act in accordance with this thought, then not only are the chances that you can, but if you act fully in accordance with it that you can and that you will is an absolute certainty. It was Vergil who, in describing the crew which in his mind would win the race, said of them: They can because they think they can. In other words, this very attitude of mind on their part will infuse a spiritual power into their bodies that will give them the strength and endurance which will enable them to win.

Then take the thought that you can, take it merely as a seed-thought, if need be, plant it in your consciousness, tend it, cultivate it, and it will gradually reach out and gather strength from all quarters. It will focus and make positive and active the spiritual force within you that is now scattered and of little avail. It will draw to itself force from without. It will draw to your aid the influence of other minds of its own nature, minds that are fearless, strong, courageous. You will thus draw to yourself and connect yourself with this order of thought. If earnest and faithful, the time will soon come when all fear will loose its hold; and instead of being an embodiment of weakness and a creature of circumstances, you will find yourself a tower of strength and a master of circumstances.

We need more faith in everyday life —faith in the power that works for good, faith in the Infinite God, and hence faith in ourselves created in His image. And however things at times may seem to go, however dark at times appearances may be, the knowledge of the fact that 'the Supreme Power has us in its charge as it has the suns and endless systems of worlds in space.' will give us the supreme faith that all is well with us, just as all is well with the world. 'Thou wilt keep in perfect peace whose mind is stayed on Thee.'

There is nothing firmer, and safer, and surer than Deity. Then, as we recognize the fact that we have it in our hands to open ourselves ever more fully to this Infinite Power, and call upon it to manifest itself in and through us, we shall find in ourselves an ever increasing sense of power. For in this way we are working in conjunction with it, and it in turn is working in conjunction with us. We are then led into the full realization of the fact that all things work together for good to those that love the good. Then the fears and forebodings that have dominated us in the past will be transmuted into faith, and faith, when rightly understood and rightly used, is a force before which nothing can stand.

Materialism leads naturally to pessimism. And how could it do otherwise? A knowledge of the Spiritual Power working in and through us as well as in and through all things, a power that works for righteousness, leads to optimism. Pessimism leads to weakness. Optimism leads to power. The one who is centered in Deity is the one who not only outrides every storm, but who through the faith, and so the conscious power that is in them, faces storm with the same calmness and serenity that they face fair weather, for they know well beforehand what the outcome will be. They know that underneath are the everlasting arms. He it is who realizes the truth of the injunction, 'Rest in the Lord, wait patiently for Him and He shall give thee thy heart's desire.' All shall be given, simply given, to him who is ready to accept it. Can anything be clearer than this?

In the degree, then, that we work in conjunction with the Supreme Power do we need the less to concern ourselves about results. To live in the full realization of this fact and all that attends it brings peace, a full, rich, abiding peace—a peace that makes the present complete, and that, going on before, brings back the assurance that as our days, so shall our strength be. The one who is thus centered, even in the face of the unrest and the turmoil about us, can realize and say:

I stay in my haste, I make delays,
For what avails this eager pace,
I stand amid eternal ways,
And what is mine shall know my face.
Asleep, awake, by night or day,
The friends I seek are seeking me.
No wind can drive my bark astray,
Nor change the tide of destiny.
The waters know their own, and draw
The brooks that spring in yonder height.
So flows the good with equal law
Unto the soul of pure delight.
The stars come nightly to the sky.
The tidal wave unto the sea,
Nor time, nor space, nor deep, nor high,
Can keep my own away from me.

Coming Into Fullness Of Power

This is the Spirit of Infinite Power, and in the degree that we open ourselves to it does power become manifest in us. With God all things are possible—that is, in conjunction with God all things are possible. The true secret of power lies in keeping one's connection with the God who worketh all things; and in the degree that we keep this connection are we able literally to rise above every conceivable limitation.

Why, then, waste time in running hither and thither to acquire power? Why waste time with this practice or that practice? Why not go directly to the mountain top itself, instead of wandering through the by-ways, in the valleys, and on the mountain sides? That man has absolute dominion, as taught in all the scriptures of the world, is true not of physical man, but of spiritual man. There are many animals, for example, larger and stronger, over which from a physical standpoint he would not have dominion, but he can gain supremacy over even these by calling into activity the higher, mental, psychic, and spiritual forces with which he is endowed.

Whatever cannot be done in the physical can be done in the spiritual. And in direct proportion as a man recognizes himself as spirit, and lives accordingly, is he able to transcend in power the man who recognizes himself merely as material. All the sacred literature of the world is teeming with examples of what we call miracles. They are not confined to any particular times or places. There is no age of miracles in distinction from any other period that may be an age of miracles. Whatever has been done in the world's history can be done again through the operation of the same laws and forces. These miracles were performed not by those who were more than men but by those who through the recognition of their oneness with God became God-men, so that the higher forces and powers worked through them.

For what, let us ask, is a miracle? Is it something supernatural? Supernatural only in the sense of being above the natural, or rather, above that which is natural to man in his ordinary state. A miracle is nothing more nor less than this One who has come into a knowledge of his true identity, of his oneness with the all-pervading Wisdom and Power, thus makes it possible for laws higher than the ordinary mind knows of to be revealed to him. These laws he makes use of, the people see the results, and by virtue of their own limitations, call them miracles and speak of the person who performs these apparently supernatural works as a supernatural being. But they as supernatural beings could themselves perform these supernatural works if they would open themselves to the recognition of the same laws, and consequently to the realization of the same possibilities and powers.

And let us also remember that the supernatural of yesterday becomes—as in the process of evolution we advance from the lower to the higher, from the more material to the more spiritual— the common and the natural of today, and what seems to be the supernatural of today becomes in the same way the natural of tomorrow, and so on through the ages.

Yes, it is the God-man who does the things that appear supernatural, the man who by virtue of his realization of the higher powers transcends the majority and so stands out among them. But any power that is possible to one human soul is possible to another. The same laws operate in every life. We can be men of power or we can be men of impotence. The moment one vitally grasps the fact that they can rise they will rise, and they can have absolutely no limitations other than the limitations they set to themselves. Cream always rises to the top. It rises simply because it is the nature of the cream to rise. We hear much said of 'environment'.

We need to realize that environment should never be allowed to make the man, but that man should always, and always can, condition the environment. When we realize this we shall find that many times it is not necessary to take ourselves out of any particular environment, because we may yet have a work to do there, but by the very force we carry with us can so affect and change matters that we shall have an entirely new set of conditions in an old environment. The same is true in regard to 'hereditary' traits and influences.

We sometimes hear the question asked, 'Can they be overcome?' Only the one who doesn't yet know themselves can ask a question such as this. If we entertain and live in the belief that they cannot be overcome, then the chances are that they will always remain. The moment, however, that we come into a realization of our true selves, and so of the tremendous powers and forces within, the powers and forces of the mind and spirit, hereditary traits and influences that are harmful in nature will begin to lessen, and will disappear with a rapidity directly in proportion to the completeness of this realization.

There is no thing we cannot overcome.
Say not thy evil instinct is inherited,
Or that some trait inborn makes thy whole life forlorn,
And calls down punishment that is not merited.
Back of thy parents and grandparents lies
The great Eternal Will: That too is thine Inheritance —strong, beautiful, divine
Sure lever of success for one who tries.
There is no noble height thou canst not climb,

> All triumphs may be thine in Time's futurity,
> If, whatso'er thy fault, thou dost not faint or halt,
> But lean upon the staff of God's security.
> Earth has no claim the soul cannot contest,
> Know thyself part of the Eternal Source,
> Naught can stand before thy spirit's force.
> The soul's Divine Inheritance is best.

Again there are many who are living far below their possibilities because they are continually handing over their individualities to others. Do you want to be a power in the world? Then be yourself. Don't class yourself, don't allow yourself to be classed among the second-hand, among the they-say people. Be true to the highest within your own soul, and then allow yourself to be governed by no customs or conventionalities or arbitrary man-made rules that are not founded upon principle. Those things that are founded upon principle will be observed by the right-minded, the right-hearted man, in any case.

Don't surrender your individuality, which is your greatest agent of power, to the customs and conventionalities that have got their life from the great mass of those who haven't enough force to preserve their individualities—those who in other words have given them over as ingredients to the 'mush of concession' which one of our greatest writers has said characterizes our modern society. If you do surrender your individuality in this way, you simply aid in increasing the undesirable conditions; in payment for this you become a slave, and the chances are that in time you will be unable to hold even the respect of those whom you in this way try to please.

If you preserve your individuality then you become a master, and if wise and discreet, your influence and power will be an aid in bringing about a higher, a better, and a more healthy set of conditions in the world. All people, moreover, will think more of you, will honor you more highly for doing this than if you show your weakness by contributing yourself to the same 'mush of concession' that so many of them are contributing themselves to. With all classes of people you will then have an influence. 'A great style of hero draws equally all classes, all extremes of society to him, till we say the very dogs believe in him.'

To be one's self is the only worthy, and by all means the only satisfactory, thing to be. 'May it not be good policy,' says one, 'to be governed sometimes by one's surroundings? What is good policy? To be yourself, first, last, and always.

> This above all—to thine own self be true,
> And it must follow, as the night the day,
> Thou canst not then be false to any man.

'When we appeal to the Supreme and our life is governed by a principle, we are not governed either by fear of public opinion or loss of others' approbation, and we may be sure that the Supreme will sustain us. If in any way we try to live to suit others we never shall suit them, and the more we try the more unreasonable and exacting do they become. The government of your life is a matter that lies entirely between God and yourself, and when your life is swayed and influenced from any other source you are on the wrong path.' When we find the kingdom within and become centered in the Infinite, then we become a law unto ourselves. When we become a law unto ourselves, then we are able to bring others to a knowledge of laws higher than they are governed or many times even enslaved by.

When we have found this center, then that beautiful simplicity, at once the charm and the power of a truly great personality, enters into our lives. Then all striving for effect — that sure indicator of weakness and a lack of genuine power — is absent. This striving for effect that is so common is always an indicator of a lack of something. It brings to mind the man who rides behind a dock-tailed horse. Conscious of the fact that there is not enough in himself to attract attention, in common with a number of other weaklings, he adopts the brutal method of having his horse's tail sawed off, that its unnatural, odd appearance may attract from people the attention that he of himself is unable to secure.

But the one who strives for effect is always fooled more than he succeeds in fooling others. The man of true wisdom and insight can always see the causes that prompt, the motives that underlie the acts of all with whom he comes in contact. 'He is great who is what he is from nature and who never reminds us of others.'

The men who are truly awake to the real powers within are the men who seem to be doing so little, yet who in reality are doing so much. They seem to be doing so little because they are working with higher agencies, and yet are doing so much because of this very fact. They do their work on the higher plane. They keep so completely their connection with the Infinite Power that It does the work for them and they are relieved of the responsibility. They are the care-less people. They are careless because it is the Infinite Power that is working through them, and with this Infinite Power they are simply cooperating.

The secret of the highest power is simply the uniting of the outer agencies of expression with the Power that works from within. Are you a painter? Then in the degree that you open yourself to the power of the forces within will you become great instead of mediocre. You can never put into permanent form inspirations higher than those that come through your own soul. In order for the higher inspirations to come through it, you must open your soul, you must open it fully to the Supreme Source of all inspiration.

Are you an orator? In the degree that you come into harmony and work in conjunction with the higher powers that will speak through you will you have the real power of molding and of moving men. If you use merely your physical agents, you will be simply a demagogue. If you open yourself so that the voice of God can speak through and use your physical agents, you will become a great and true orator, great and true in just the degree that you so open yourself.

Are you a singer? Then open yourself and let the God within forth in the spirit of song. You will find it a thousand times easier than all your long and studied practice without this, and other things being equal, there will come to you a power of song so enchanting and so enrapturing that its influence upon all who hear will be irresistible.

When my cabin or tent has been pitched during the summer on the edge or in the midst of a forest, I have sometimes lain awake on my cot in the early morning, just as the day was beginning to break. Silence at first. Then an intermittent chirp here and there. And as the unfolding tints of the dawn became faintly perceptible, these grew more and more frequent, until by and by the whole forest seemed to burst forth in one grand chorus of song. Wonderful! wonderful! It seemed as if the very trees, as if every grass-blade, as if the bushes, the very sky above and the earth beneath, had part in this wonderful symphony. Then, as I have listened as it went on and on, I have thought, What a study in the matter of song! If we could but learn from the birds. If we could but open ourselves to the same powers and allow them to pour forth in us, what singers, and what movers of men we might have! Nay, what singers and what movers of men we would have!

Do you know the circumstances under which Mr Sankey sang for the first time 'The Ninety and Nine'? Says one of our able journalists: 'At a great meeting recently, Mr Ira D. Sankey, before singing "The Ninety and Nine," which, perhaps, of all his compositions is the one that has brought him the most fame, gave an account of its birth. Leaving Glasgow for Edinburgh with Mr Moody, he stopped at a paper-stall and bought a penny religious paper. Glancing over it as they rode in the train, his eye fell on a few little verses in the corner of the page. Turning to Mr Moody, he said, "I've found my hymn." But Mr Moody was engaged and did not hear a word. Mr Sankey did not find time to make a tune for the verses, so he pasted them in his music scrapbook.

'One day they had an unusually impressive meeting in Edinburgh, in which Dr Bonar had spoken with great effect on "The Good Shepherd." At the close of the address Mr Moody beckoned to his partner to sing. He thought of nothing but the Twenty-third Psalm, but that he had sung so often. His second thought was to sing the verses he had found in the newspaper, but the third thought was, how could it be done when he had no tune. Then a fourth thought came, and that was to sing them anyway. He put the verses before him, touched the keys of the organ, opened his mouth and sang, not knowing where he was going to come out. He finished the first verse amid profound silence. He took a long breath and wondered if he could sing the second the same way. He tried and succeeded; after that it was easy to sing it. When he finished the hymn the meeting was all broken down and the throngs were crying. Mr Sankey says it was the intense moment of his life. Mr Moody said he never heard a song like it. It was sung at every meeting, and was soon going over the world.'

When we open ourselves to the highest inspirations they never fail us. When we fail to do this we fail in attaining the highest results, whatever the undertaking.

Are you a writer? Then remember that the one great precept underlying all successful literary work is, Look into thine own heart and write. Be true. Be fearless. Be loyal to the promptings of your own soul. Remember that an author can never write more than he themselves are. If he would write more, then they must be more. They are simply their own amanuensis. They in a sense write themselves into their book. They can put no more into it than they themselves are.

If he is one of a great personality, strong in purpose, deep in feeling, open always to the highest inspirations, a certain indefinable something gets into their pages that makes them breathe forth a vital, living power, a power so great that each reader gets the same inspirations as those that spoke through the author. That which is written between the lines is many times more than that which is written in the lines. It is the spirit of the author that engenders this power. It is this that gives that extra twenty-five or thirty per cent that takes a book out of the class called medium and lifts it into the class called superior, that extra per cent that makes it the one of the hundred that is truly successful, while the ninety-nine never see more than their first edition.

It is this same spiritual power that the author of a great personality puts into their work that causes it to go so rapidly from reader to reader; for the way that any book circulates is mainly from personal recommendation —any book that reaches a large circulation. It is this that many times causes a single reader, in view of its value to themselves, to purchase numbers of copies for others. 'A good poem,' says Emerson, 'goes about the world offering itself to reasonable men, who read it with joy and carry it to their reasonable neighbors. Thus it draws to it the wise and generous souls, confirming their secret thoughts, and through their sympathy really publishing itself.'

This is the type of author who writes not with the thought of having what they write become literature, but they write with the sole thought of reaching the hearts of the people, giving them something of vital value, something that will broaden, sweeten, enrich, and beautify their lives; that will lead them to the finding of the higher life and with it the higher powers and the higher joys. It nearly always happens, however, that if they succeed in thus reaching the people, the becoming literature part somehow takes care of itself, and far better than if they aimed for it directly.

The one, on the other hand, who fears to depart from beaten paths, who allows themselves to be bound by arbitrary rules, limits their own creative powers in just the degree that then allow themselves to be so bound. 'My book,' says one of the greatest of modern authors, 'shall smell of the pines and resound with the hum of insects. The swallow over my window shall interweave that thread or straw he carries in his bill into my web also.' Far better, gentle sage, to have it smell of the pines and resound with the hum of insects than to have it sound of the rules that a smaller type of man gets by studying the works of a few great, fearless writers like yourself, and formulating from what he thus gains a handbook of rhetoric. 'Of no use are the men who study to do exactly as was done before, who can never understand that today is a new day.'

When Shakespeare is charged with debts to his authors, Landor replies, 'Yet he was more original than his originals. He breathed upon dead bodies and brought them into life.' This is the type of man who doesn't move the world's way, but who moves the world his way. I had rather be an amanuensis of the Infinite God, as it is my privilege literally to be, than a slave to the formulated rules of any rhetorician, or to the opinions of any critic.

Oh, the people, the people over and over! Let me give something to them that will lighten the everyday struggles of our common life, something that will add a little sweetness here, a little hope there, something that will make more thoughtful, kind, and gentle this thoughtless, animal-natured man, something that will awaken into activity the dormant powers of this timid, shrinking little woman, powers that when awakened will be irresistible in their influence and that will surprise even herself. Let me give something that will lead each one to the knowledge of the divinity of every human soul, something that will lead each one to the conscious realization of their own divinity, with all its attendant riches, and glories, and powers —let me succeed in doing this, and I can then well afford to be careless as to whether the critics praise or whether they blame. If it is blame, then under these circumstances it is as the cracking of a few dead sticks on the ground below, compared to the matchless music that the soft spring gale is breathing through the great pine forest.

Are you a minister, or a religious teacher of any kind? Then in the degree that you free yourself from the man-made theological dogmas that have held and that are holding and limiting so many, and in the degree that you open yourself to the Divine Breath, will you be one who will speak with authority. In the degree that you do this will you study the prophets less and be in the way of becoming a prophet yourself. The way is open for you exactly the same as it has ever been open for anyone.

If when born into the world you came into a family of the English-speaking race, then in all probability you are a Christian. To be a Christian is to be a follower of the teachings of Jesus, the Christ; to live in harmony with the same laws He lived in harmony with: in brief, to live His life. The great central fact of His teaching was this conscious union of man with the Father. It was the complete realization of this oneness with the Father on His part that made Jesus the Christ. It was through this that He attained to the power He attained to, that He spake as never man spake.

He never claimed for Himself anything that He did not claim equally for all mankind. 'The mighty works performed by Jesus were not exceptional, they were the natural and necessary concomitants of His state; He declared them to be in accordance with unvarying order; He spoke of them as no unique performances, but as the outcome of a state to which all might attain if they chose. As a teacher and demonstrator of truth, according to His own confession, He did nothing for the purpose of proving His solitary divinity.... The life and triumph of Jesus formed an epoch in the history of the race. His coming and victory marked a new era in human affairs; He introduced a new because a more complete ideal to the earth, and when His three most intimate companions saw in some measure what the new life really signified, they fell to the earth, speechless with awe and admiration.'

By coming into this complete realization of His oneness with the Father, by mastering, absolutely mastering every circumstance that crossed His path through life, even to the death of the body, and by pointing out to us the great laws which are the same for us as they were for Him, He has given us an ideal of life, an ideal for us to attain to here and now, that we could not have without Him. One has conquered first, all conquer afterward. By completely realizing it first for Himself, and then by pointing out to others this great law of the at-one-ment with the Father, He has become the world's greatest Savior.

Don't mistake His mere person for His life and His teachings, an error that has been made in connection with nearly all great teachers by their disciples over and over again. And if you have been among the number who have been preaching a dead Christ, then for humanity's sake, for Christ's sake, for God's sake, and I speak most reverently, don't steal the people's time any longer, don't waste your own time more, in giving them stones in place of bread, dead form for the spirit of living truth. In His own words, 'let the dead bury their dead.' Come out from among them. Teach as did Jesus, the living Christ. Teach as did Jesus, the Christ within. Find this in all its transcendent beauty and power, find it as Jesus found it, then you also will be one who will speak with authority. Then you will be able to lead large numbers of others to its finding. This is the pearl of great price.

It is the type of preacher whose soul has never as yet even perceived the vital spirit of the teaching of Jesus, and who as a consequence instead of giving this to the people, is giving them old forms and dogmas and speculations, who is emptying our churches. This is the type whose chief efforts seem to be in getting men ready to die. The Germans have a saying, Never go to the second thing first. We need men who will teach us first how to live. Living quite invariably precedes dying. This also is true, that when we once know how to live, and live in accordance with what we know, then the dying, as we term it, will in a wonderfully beautiful manner take care of itself. It is in fact the only way in which it can be taken care of.

It is on account of this emptying of our churches, for the reason that the people are tiring ot mere husks, that many short-sighted people are frequently heard to say that religion is dying out. Religion dying out? How can anything die before it is really born? And so far as the people are concerned, religion is just being born, or rather they are just awaking to a vital, every-day religion. We are just beginning to get beyond the mere letter into its real, vital spirit. Religion dying out? Impossible even to conceive of. Religion is as much a part of the human soul as the human soul is a part of God. And as long as God and the human soul exist religion will never die.

Much of the dogma, the form, the ceremony, the mere letter that has stood as religion—and honestly, many times, let us be fair enough to say—this, thank God, is rapidly dying out, and never so rapidly as it is today. By two methods it is dying. There is, first, a large class of people tired of or even nauseated with it all, who conscientiously prefer to have nothing rather than this. They are simply abandoning it, as a tree abandons its leaves when the early winter comes.

There is, second, a large class in whom the Divine Breath is stirring, who are finding the Christ within in all its matchless beauty and redeeming power. And this new life is pushing off the old, the same as in the spring the newly awakened life in the tree pushes off the old, lifeless leaves that have clung on during the winter, to make place for the new ones. And the way this old dead-leaf religion is being pushed off on every hand is indeed most interesting and inspiring to witness.

Let the places of those who have been emptying our churches by reason of their attempts to give stones for bread, husks and chaff for the life-giving grain, let their places be taken even for but a few times by those who are open and alive to these higher inspirations, and then let us again question those who feel that religion is dying out. 'It is the live coal that kindles others, not the dead.' Let their places be taken by those who have caught the inspiration of the Divine Breath, who as a consequence have a message of mighty value and import for the people, who by virtue of this same fact are able to present it with a beauty and a power so enrapturing that it takes captive the soul.

Then we will find that the churches that today are dotted here and there with a few dozen people will be filled to overflowing, and there will not be even room enough for all who would enter. 'Let the shell perish that the pearl may appear.' We need no new revelations as yet. We need simply to find the vital spirit of those we already have. Then in due time, when we are ready for them, new ones will come, but not before.

'What the human soul, all the world over, needs,' says John Pulsford, 'is not to be harangued, however eloquently, about the old, accepted religion, but to be permeated, charmed, and taken captive by a warmer and more potent Breath of God than they ever felt before. And I should not be true to my personal experience if I did not bear testimony that this Divine Breath is as exquisitely adapted to the requirements of the soul's nature as a June morning to the planet. Nor does the morning breath leave the trees freer to delight themselves and develop themselves under its influence than the Breath of God allows each human mind to unfold according to its genius. Nothing stirs the central wheel of the soul like the Breath of God. The whole man is quickened, his senses are new senses, his emotions new emotions, his reason, his affections, his imagination, are all new-born.

The change is greater than he knows, he marvels at the powers in himself which the Breath is opening and calling forth. He finds his nature to be an unutterable thing; he is sure therefore that the future must have inconceivable surprises in store. And herein lies the evidence, which I commend to my readers, of the existence of God, and of the Eternal human Hope. Let God's Breath kindle new spring-time in the soul, start into life its deeply buried germs, lead in heaven's summer, you will then have as clear evidence of God from within as you have of the universe from without. Indeed, your internal experience of life, and illimitable Hope in God will be nearer to you, and more prevailing, than all your external and superficial experience of nature and the world.'

There is but one source of power in the universe. Whatever then you are, painter, orator, musician, writer, religious teacher, or whatever it may be, know that to catch and take captive the secret of power is so to work in conjunction with the Infinite Power, in order that it may continually work and manifest through you. If you fail in doing this, you fail in everything. If you fail in doing this, your work, whatever it may be, will be third or fourth rate, possibly at times second rate, but it positively never can be first rate Absolutely impossible will it be for you ever to become a master.

Whatever estimate you put upon yourself will determine the effectiveness of your work along any line. As long as you live merely in the physical and the intellectual, you set limitations to yourself that will hold you as long as you so live. When, however, you come into the realization of your oneness with the Infinite Life and Power, and open yourself that it may work through you, you will find that you have entered upon an entirely new phase of life, and that an ever increasing power will be yours. Then it will be true that your strength will be as the strength of ten because your heart is pure.

> O God! I am one forever
> With Thee by the glory of birth.
> The celestial powers proclaim it
> To the utmost bounds of the earth.
> I think of this birthright immortal,
> And my being expands like a rose,
> As an odorous cloud of incense
> Around and above me flows.
> A glorious song of rejoicing
> In an innermost spirit I hear,
> And it sounds like heavenly voices,
> In a chorus divine and clear.
> And I feel a power uprising,
> Like the power of an embryo god.
> With a glorious wall it surrounds me,
> And lifts me up from the sod.

Plenty Of All Things
The Law Of Prosperity

This is the Spirit of Infinite Plenty, the Power that has brought, that is continually bringing, all things into expression in material form. He who lives in the realization of his oneness with this Infinite Power becomes a magnet to attract to himself a continual supply of whatsoever things he desires.

If one holds themselves in the thought of poverty they will be poor, and the chances are that they will remain in poverty. If one holds themselves, whatever present conditions may be, continually in the thought of prosperity, they set into operation forces that will sooner or later bring them into prosperous conditions. The law of attraction works unceasingly throughout the universe, and the one great and never changing fact in connection with it is, as we have found, that like attracts like. If we are one with this Infinite Power, this source of all things, then in the degree that we live in the realization of this oneness, in that degree do we actualize in ourselves a power that will bring to us an abundance of all things that it is desirable for us to have. In this way we come into possession of a power whereby we can actualize at all times those conditions that we desire.

As all truth exists now, and awaits simply our perception of it, so all things necessary for present needs exist now, and await simply the power in us to appropriate them. God holds all things in His hands. His constant word is, My child, acknowledge me in all your ways, and in the degree that you do this, in the degree that you live this, then what is mine is yours. Jehovah-jireh—the Lord will provide. 'He giveth to all men liberally and upbraideth not.' He giveth liberally to all men who put themselves in the right attitude to receive from Him. He forces no good things upon anyone.

The old and somewhat prevalent idea of godliness and poverty has absolutely no basis for its existence, and the sooner we get away from it the better. It had its birth in the same way that the idea of asceticism came into existence, when the idea prevailed that there was necessarily a warfare between the flesh and the spirit. It had its origin therefore in the minds of those who had a distorted, a one-sided view of life. True godliness is in a sense the same as true wisdom. The one who is truly wise, and who uses the forces and powers with which they are endowed, to them the great universe always opens her treasure house.

The supply is always equal to the demand -equal to the demand when the demand is rightly, wisely made. When one comes into the realization of these higher laws, then the fear of want ceases to tyrannize over them.

Are you out of a situation? Let the fear that you will not get another take hold of and dominate you, and the chances are that it may be a long time before you will get another, or the one that you do get may be a very poor one indeed. Whatever the circumstances, you must realize that you have within you forces and powers that you can set into operation that will triumph over any and all apparent or temporary losses. Set these forces into operation and you will then be placing a magnet that will draw to you a situation that may be far better than the one you have lost, and the time may soon come when you will be even thankful that you lost the old one.

Recognize, working in and through you, the same Infinite Power that creates and governs all things in the universe, the same Infinite Power that governs the endless systems of worlds in space. Send out your thought—thought is a force, and it has occult power of unknown proportions when rightly used and wisely directed—send out your thought that the right situation or the right work will come to you at the right time, in the right way, and that you will recognize it when it comes. Hold to this thought, never allow it to weaken, hold to it, and continually water it with firm expectation.

You in this way put your advertisement into a psychical, a spiritual newspaper, a paper that has not a limited circulation, but one that will make its way not only to the utmost bounds of the earth, but of the very universe itself. It is an advertisement, moreover, which if rightly placed on your part, will be far more effective than any advertisement you could possibly put into any printed sheet, no matter what claims are made in regard to its being 'the great advertising medium'. In the degree that you come into this realization and live in harmony with the higher laws and forces, in that degree will you be able to do this effectively.

If you wish to look through the 'want' columns of the newspapers, then do not do it in the ordinary way. Put the higher forces into operation and thus place it on a higher basis. As you take up the paper, take this attitude of mind: If there is here an advertisement that it will be well for me to reply to, the moment I come to it I will recognize it. Affirm this, believe it, expect it. If you do this in full faith, you will somehow feel the intuition the moment you come to the right one, and this intuition will be nothing more nor less than your own soul speaking to you. When it speaks then act at once.

If you get the situation and it does not prove to be exactly what you want, if you feel that you are capable of filling a better one, then the moment you enter upon it take the attitude of mind that this situation is the stepping-stone that will lead you to one that will be still better.

Hold this thought steadily, affirm it, believe it, expect it, and all the time be faithful, absolutely faithful to the situation in which you are at present placed. If you are not faithful to it then the chances are that it will not be the stepping-stone to something better, but to something poorer. If you are faithful to it, the time may soon come when you will be glad and thankful, when you will rejoice that you lost your old position.

This is the law of prosperity: When apparent adversity comes, be not cast down by it, but make the best of it, and always look forward for better things, for conditions more prosperous. To hold yourself in this attitude of mind is to set into operation subtle, silent, and irresistible forces that sooner or later will actualize in material form that which is today merely an idea. But ideas have occult power, and ideas, when rightly planted and rightly tended, are the seeds that actualize material conditions.

Never give a moment to complaint, but utilize the time that would otherwise be spent in this way in looking forward and actualizing the conditions you desire. Suggest prosperity to yourself. See yourself in a prosperous condition. Affirm that you will before be in a prosperous condition. Affirm it calmly and quietly, but strongly and confidently. Believe it, believe it absolutely. Expect it, keep it continually watered with expectation. You thus make yourself a magnet to attract the things that you desire.

Don't be afraid to suggest, to affirm these things, for by so doing you put forth an ideal which will begin to clothe itself in material form. In this way you are utilizing agents among the most subtle and powerful in the universe. If you are particularly desirous for anything that you feel it is good and right for you to have, something that will broaden your life or that will increase your usefulness to others, simply hold the thought that at the right time, in the right way, and through the right instrumentality, there will come to you or there will open up for you the way whereby you can attain what you desire.

I know of a young lady who a short time ago wanted some money very badly. She wanted it for a good purpose; she saw no reason why she shouldn't have it. She is one who has come into an understanding of the power of the interior forces. She took and held herself in the attitude of mind we have just pointed out. In the morning she entered into the silence for a few moments. In this way she brought herself into a more complete harmony with the higher powers. Before the day closed a gentleman called, a member of a family with which she was acquainted. He asked her if she would do for the family some work that they wanted done.

She was a little surprised that they should ask her to do this particular kind of work, but she said to herself, 'Here is a call. I will respond and see what it will lead to.' She undertook the work. She did it well. When she had completed it there was put into her hands an amount of money far beyond what she had expected. She felt that it was an amount too large for the work she had done. She protested. They replied, 'No; you have done us a service that transcends in value the amount we offer to pay you.' The sum thus received was more than sufficient for the work she wished to accomplish.

This is but one of many instances in connection with the wise and effective use of the higher powers. It also carries a lesson —Don't fold your hands and expect to see things drop into your lap, but set into operation the higher forces and then take hold of the first thing that offers itself. Do what your hands find to do, and do it well. If this work is not thoroughly satisfactory to you, then affirm, believe, and expect that it is the agency that will lead you to something better. 'The basis for attracting the best of all the world can give to you is first to surround, own, and live in these things in mind, or what is falsely called imagination. All so-called imaginings are realities and forces of unseen element. Live in mind in a palace and gradually palatial surroundings will gravitate to you. But so living is not pining, or longing, or complainingly wishing. It is when you are "down in the world", calmly and persistently seeing yourself as up. It is when you are now compelled to eat from a tin plate, regarding that tin plate as only the certain step to one of silver. It is not envying and growling at other people who have silver plate. That growling is just so much capital stock taken from the bank account of mental force.'

A friend who knows the power of the interior forces, and whose life is guided in every detail by them, has given a suggestion in this form. When you are in the arms of the bear, even though he is hugging you, look him in the face and laugh, but all the time keep your eye on the bull. If you allow all of your attention to be given to the work of the bear, the bull may get entirely out of your sight. In other words, if you yield to adversity the chances are that it will master you, but if you recognize in yourself the powers of mastery over conditions then adversity will yield to you, and will be changed into prosperity. If when it comes you calmly and quietly recognize it, and use the time that might otherwise be spent in regrets, and fears, and forebodings, in setting into operation the powerful forces within you, it will soon take its leave.

Faith, absolute dogmatic faith, is the only law of true success. When we recognize the fact that a man carries their success or failure with them, and that it does not depend upon outside conditions, we shall come into the possession of powers that will quickly change outside conditions into agencies that make for success. When we come into this higher realization and bring our lives into complete harmony with the higher laws, we shall then be able so to focus and direct the awakened interior forces, that they will go out and return laden with that for which they are sent. We shall then be great enough to attract success, and it will not always be apparently just a little way ahead. We can then establish in ourselves a center so strong that instead of running hither and thither for this or that, we can stay at home and draw to us the conditions we desire. If we firmly establish and hold to this center, things will seem continually to come our way.

The majority of people of the modern world are looking for things that are practical and that can be utilized in everyday life. The more carefully we examine into the laws underlying the great truths we are considering, the more we shall find that they are not only eminently practical, but in a sense, and in the deepest and truest sense, they are the only practical things there are.

There are people who continually pride themselves upon being exceedingly 'practical'; but many times those who of themselves think nothing about this are the most practical people the world knows. And, on the other hand, those who take great pride in speaking of their own practicality are often the least practical. Or again, in some ways they may be practical, but so far as life in its is concerned, they are absurdly impractical.

What profit, for example, can there be for the man who, materially speaking, though they have gained the whole world, have never yet become acquainted with their own soul? There are multitudes of men all about us who are entirely missing the real life, people who have not learned even the A, B, C of true living. Slaves they are, abject slaves to their temporary material accumulations. Men who, thinking they possess their wealth, are on the contrary completely possessed by it. Men whose lives are comparatively barren in service to those about them and to the world at large. Men who when they can no longer hold the body—the agency by means of which they are related to the material world—will go out poor indeed, pitiably poor. Unable to take even the smallest particle of their accumulations with them, they will enter upon the other form of life naked and destitute.

The kindly deeds, the developed traits of character, the realized powers of the soul, the real riches of the inner life and unfoldment, all those things that become our real and eternal possessions, have been given no place in their lives, and so of the real things of life they are destitute. Nay, many times worse than destitute. We must not suppose that habits once formed are any more easily broken off in the other form of life than they are in this. If one voluntarily grows a certain mania here, we must not suppose that the mere dropping of the body makes all conditions perfect. All is law, all is cause and effect. As we sow, so shall we also reap, not only in this life but in all lives.

He who is enslaved with the sole desire for material possessions here will continue to be enslaved even after he can no longer retain his body. Then, moreover, he will have not even the means of gratifying his desires. Dominated by this habit, he will be unable to set his affections, for a time at least, upon other things, and the desire, without the means of gratifying it, will be doubly torturing to him. Perchance this torture may be increased by his seeing the accumulations he thought were his now being scattered and wasted by spend thrifts. He wills his property, as we say, to others, but he can have no word as to its use.

How foolish, then, for us to think that any material possessions are ours. How absurd, for example, for one to fence off a number of acres of God's earth and say they are his. Nothing is ours that we cannot retain. The things that come into our hands come not for the purpose of being possessed, as we say, much less for the purpose of being hoarded. They come into our hands to be used, to be used wisely. We are stewards merely, and as stewards we shall be held accountable for the way we use whatever is entrusted to us. That great law of compensation that runs through all life is wonderfully exact in its workings, although we may not always fully comprehend it, or even recognize it when it operates in connection with ourselves.

The one who has come into the realization of the higher life no longer has a desire for the accumulation of enormous wealth, any more than he has a desire for any other excess. In the degree that they come into the recognition of the fact that they are wealthy within, external wealth becomes less important in their estimation. When they come into the realization of the fact that there is a source within from which they can put forth a power to call to them, and actualize in their hands at any time, a sufficient supply for all their needs they no longer burden themselves with vast material accumulations that require their constant care and attention, and thus take their time and their thought from the real things of life. In other words, they first find the kingdom, and they realize that when they have found this all other things follow in full measure.

It is as hard for a rich man to enter into the kingdom of heaven, said the Master—He who having nothing had everything—as it is for a camel to pass through the eye of a needle. In other words, if a man give all his time to the accumulation, the hoarding of outward material possessions far beyond what he can possibly ever use, what time has he for the finding of that wonderful kingdom which, when found, brings all else with it. Which is better, to have millions and to have the burden of taking care of it all—for the one always involves the other—or to come into the knowledge of such laws and forces that every need will be supplied in good time, to know that no good thing shall be withheld, to know that we have it in our power to make the supply always equal to the demand?

The one who enters into the realm of this higher knowledge never cares to bring upon themselves the species of insanity that has such a firm hold upon so many in the world today. They avoid it as they would avoid any loathsome disease of the body. When we come into the realization of the higher powers, we will then be able to give more attention to the real life, instead of giving so much to the piling up of vast possessions that hamper rather than help it. It is the medium ground that brings the true solution here, as it is in all phases of life.

Wealth beyond a certain amount cannot be used, and when it cannot be used it then becomes a hindrance rather than an aid, a curse rather than a blessing. All about us are persons with lives now stunted and dwarfed which might be made rich and beautiful, filled with a perennial joy, if they would begin wisely to use that which they have spent the greater portion of their lives in accumulating.

The man who accumulates during their entire life, and who even leaves all when they go out for 'benevolent purposes', comes far short of the ideal life. It is but a poor excuse of a life. It is not especially commendable in me to give a pair of old, worn-out shoes that I shall never use again to another who is in need of shoes. But it is commendable, if indeed doing anything we ought to do can be spoken of as being commendable, it is commendable for me to give a good pair of strong shoes to the man who in the midst of a severe winter is practically shoeless, the man who is exerting every effort to earn an honest living and thereby take care of his family's needs. And if in giving the shoes I also give myself, he then has a double gift, and I a double blessing.

There is no wiser use that those who have great accumulations can make of them than wisely to put them into life, into character, day by day while they live. In this way their lives will be continually enriched and increased. The time will come when it will be regarded as a disgrace for a man to die and leave vast accumulations behind them. Many a person is living in a palace today who in the real life is poorer than many a one who has not even a roof to cover him.

A man may own and live in a palace, but the palace for them may be a poorhouse still.

Moth and rust are nature's wise provisions—God's methods—for disintegrating and scattering, in this way getting ready for use in new forms that which is hoarded and consequently serving no use. There is also a great law continually operating the effects of which are to dwarf and deaden the powers of true enjoyment, as well as all the higher faculties, of the one who hoards.

Multitudes of people are continually keeping away from them higher and better things because they are forever clinging on to the old. If they would use and pass on the old, room would be made for new things to come. Hoarding always brings loss in one form or another. Using, wisely using, brings an ever renewing gain. If the tree should as ignorantly and as greedily hold on to this year's leaves when they have served their purpose, where would be the full and beautiful new life that will be put forth in the spring? Gradual decay and finally death would be the result. If the tree is already dead, then it may perhaps be well enough for it to cling on to the old, for no new leaves will come. But as long as the life in the tree is active, it is necessary that it rid itself of the old ones, that room may be made for the new.

Opulence is the law of the universe, an abundant supply for every need if nothing is put in the way of its coming. The natural and the normal life for us is this —to have such a fullness of life and power by living so continually in the realization of our oneness with the Infinite Life and Power that we find ourselves in the constant possession of an abundant supply of all things needed. Then not by hoarding, but by wisely using and ridding ourselves of things as they come, an ever renewing supply will be ours, a supply far better adapted to present needs than the old could possibly be. In this way we not only come into possession of the richest treasures of the Infinite Good ourselves, but we also become open channels through which they can flow to others.

How Men Have Become Prophets, Seers, Sages, And Saviors

I Have tried thus far to deal fairly with you in presenting these vital truths, and have spoken of everything on the basis of our own reason and insight. It has been my aim to base nothing on the teachings of others, though they may be the teachings of those inspired. Let us now look for a moment at these same great truths in the light of the thoughts and the teachings as put forth by some of the world's great thinkers and inspired teachers.

The sum and substance of the thought presented in these pages is, you will remember, that the great central fact in human life is the coming into a conscious, vital realization of our oneness with the Infinite Life, and the opening of ourselves fully to this divine inflow. I and the Father are one, said the Master. In this we see how He recognized His oneness with the Father's life. Again He said, The words that I speak unto you I speak not of Myself: but the Father that dwelleth in Me, He doeth the works. In this we see how clearly He recognized the fact that He of Himself could do nothing, only as He worked in conjunction with the Father. Again, My Father works and I work. In other words, my Father sends the power, I open Myself to it, and work in conjunction with it.

Again He said, Seek ye first the kingdom of God and His righteousness, and all these things shall be added unto you. And He left us not in the dark as to exactly what He meant by this, for again He said, Say not Lo here nor lo there, know ye not that the kingdom of heaven is within you? According to His teaching, the kingdom of God and the kingdom of heaven were one and the same. If, then, His teaching is that the kingdom of heaven is within us, do we not clearly see that, putting it in other words, His injunction is nothing more nor less than, Come ye into a conscious realization of your oneness with the Father's life. As you realize this oneness you find the kingdom and when you find this, all things else shall follow.

The story of the prodigal son is another beautiful illustration of this same great teaching of the Master. After the prodigal had spent everything, after he had wandered in all the realms of the physical senses in the pursuit of happiness and pleasure, and found that this did not satisfy but only brought him to the level of the animal creation, he then came to his senses and said, I will arise and go to my Father. In other words, after all these wanderings, his own soul at length spoke to him and said.

You are not a mere animal. You are your Father's child. Arise and go to your Father, who holds all things in His hands. Again, the Master said, Call no man your father upon the earth: for one is your Father, which is in heaven. Here He recognized the fact that the real life is direct from the life of God. Our fathers and our mothers are the agents that give us the bodies, the houses in which we live, but the real life comes from the Infinite Source of Life, God, who is our Father.

One day word was brought to the Master that His mother and His brethren were without wishing to speak with Him. Who is My mother and who are My brethren? said He. Whosoever shall do the will of My Father which is in heaven, the same is My brother, and My sister, and mother.

Many people are greatly enslaved by what we term ties of relationship. It is well, however, for us to remember that our true relatives are not necessarily those who are connected with us by ties of blood. Our truest relatives are those who are nearest akin to us in mind, in soul, in spirit. Our nearest relatives may be those living on the opposite side of the globe—people whom we may never have seen as yet, but to whom we will yet be drawn, either in this form of life or in another, through that ever working and never failing Law of Attraction.

When the Master gave the injunction, Call no man your father upon the earth: for one is your Father, which is in heaven, He here gave us the basis for that grand conception of the fatherhood of God. And if God is equally the Father of all, then we have here the basis for the brotherhood of man. But there is, in a sense, a conception still higher than this, namely, the oneness of man and God, and hence the oneness of the whole human race. When we realize this fact, then we clearly see how in the degree that we come into the realization of our oneness with the Infinite Life, and so every step that we make Godward, we aid in lifting all mankind up to this realization, and enable them, in turn, to make a step Godward.

The Master again pointed out our true relations with the Infinite Life when He said, Except ye become as little children ye shall not enter into the kingdom of heaven. When He said, Man shall not live by bread alone, but by every word that proceedeth out of the mouth of God, He gave utterance to a truth of far greater import than we have as yet commenced fully to grasp. Here He taught that even the physical life cannot be maintained by material food alone, but that one's connection with this Infinite Source determines to a very great extent the condition of even the bodily structure and activities. Blessed are the pure in heart for they shall see God. In other words, blessed are they who in all the universe recognize only God, for by such God shall be seen.

Said the great Hindu sage, Manu, He who in his own soul perceives the Supreme Soul in all beings, and acquires equanimity toward them all, attains the highest bliss. It was Athanasius who said, Even we may become Gods walking about in the flesh. The same great truth we are considering is the one that runs through the life and the teachings of Gautama, he who became the Buddha. People are in bondage, said he, because they have not yet removed the idea of I. To do away with all sense of separateness, and to recognize the oneness of the self with the Infinite, is the spirit that breathes through all his teachings. Running through the lives of all the mediaeval mystics was this same great truth —union with God.

Then, coming nearer to our own time, we find the highly illumined seer, Emanuel Swedenborg, pointing out the great laws in connection with what he termed the divine influx, and how we may open ourselves more fully to its operations. The great central fact in the religion and worship of the Friends is the inner light—God in the soul of man speaking directly in just the degree that the soul is opened to Him. The inspired one, the seer who when with us lived at Concord, recognized the same great truth when he said, We are all inlets to the great sea of life. And it was by opening himself so fully to its inflow that he became one inspired.

All through the world's history we find that the men who have entered into the realm of true wisdom and power, and hence into the realm of true peace and joy, have lived in harmony with this Higher Power. David was strong and powerful and his soul burst forth in praise and adoration in just the degree that he listened to the voice of God, and lived in accordance with his higher promptings. Whenever he failed to do this we hear his soul crying out in anguish and lamentation. The same is true of every nation or people. When the Israelites acknowledged God and followed according to His leadings they were prosperous, contented, and powerful, and nothing could prevail against them. When they depended upon their own strength alone and failed to recognize God as the source of their strength, we find them overcome, in bondage, or despair.

A great immutable law underlies the truth, Blessed are they that hear the word of God and do it. Then follows all. We are wise in the degree that we live according to the higher light.

All the prophets, seers, sages, and saviors in the world's history became what they became, and consequently had the powers they had, through an entirely natural process. They all recognized and came into the conscious realization of their oneness with the Infinite Life. God is no respecter of persons.

He does not create prophets, seers, sages, and saviors as such. He creates men. But here and there one recognizes their true identity, recognizes the oneness of their life with the Source whence it came. They live in the realization of this oneness, and in turn becomes a prophet, seer, sage, or savior. Neither is God a respecter of races or of nations. He has no chosen people; but here and there a race or nation becomes a respecter of God and hence lives the life of a chosen people.

There has been no age or place of miracles in distinction from any other age or place. What we term miracles have abounded in all places and at all times where conditions have been made for them. They are being performed today, just as much as they ever have been, when the laws governing them are respected. Mighty men, we are told they were, mighty men who walked with God; and in the words 'who walked with God' lies the secret of the words 'mighty men'. Cause, effect.

The Lord never prospers any man, but the man prospers because he acknowledges the Lord, and lives in accordance with the higher laws. Solomon was given the opportunity of choosing whatever he desired, his better judgment prevailed and he chose wisdom. But when he chose wisdom he found that it included all else beside. We are told that God hardened Pharaoh's heart. I don't believe it. God never hardens any one's heart. Pharaoh hardened his own heart and God was blamed for it. But when Pharaoh hardened his heart and disobeyed the voice of God, the plagues came. Again, cause, effect. Had he, on the contrary, listened —in other words, had he opened himself to and obeyed the voice of God —the plagues would not have come.

We can be our own best friends or we can be our own worst enemies. In the degree that we become friends to the highest and best within us, we become friends to all; and in the degree that we become enemies to the highest and best within us, do we become enemies to all. In the degree that we open ourselves to the higher powers and let them manifest through us, then by the very inspirations we carry with us do we become in a sense the saviors of our fellow-men, and in this way we all are, or may become, the saviors one of another. In this way you may become, indeed, one of the world's redeemers.

The Basic Principle Of All Religions
The Universal Religion

The great truth we are considering is the fundamental principle running through all religions. We find it in every one. In regard to it all agree. It is, moreover, a great truth in regard to which all people can agree, whether they belong to the same or to different religions. People always quarrel about the trifles, about their personal views of minor insignificant points. They always come together in the presence of great fundamental truths, the threads of which run through all. The quarrels are in connection with the lower self, the agreements are in connection with the higher self.

A place may have its factions that quarrel and fight among themselves, but let a great calamity come upon the land, flood, famine, pestilence, and these little personal differences are entirely forgotten and all work shoulder to shoulder in the one great cause. The changing, the evolving self gives rise to quarrels; the permanent, the soul self unites all in the highest efforts of love and service.

Patriotism is a beautiful thing; it is well for me to love my country, but why should I love my own country more than I love all others? If I love my own and hate others I then show my limitations, and my patriotism will stand the test not even for my own. If I love my own country and in the same way love all other countries, then I show the largeness of my nature, and a patriotism of this kind is noble and always to be relied upon.

The view of God in regard to which we are agreed, that He is the Infinite Spirit of Life and Power that is at the back of all, that is working in and through all, that is the life of all, is a matter in regard to which all men, all religions can agree. With this view there can be no infidels or atheists. There are atheists and infidels in connection with many views that are held concerning God, and thank God there are! Even devout and earnest people among us attribute things to God that no respectable men would permit to be attributed to themselves. This view is satisfying to those who cannot see how God can be angry with His children, jealous, vindictive. A display of these qualities always lessens our for men, and still we attribute them to God.

The earnest, sincere heretic is one of the greatest friends true religion can have. Heretics are among God's greatest servants. They are among the true servants of mankind. Christ was one of the greatest heretics the world has ever known. He allowed Himself to be bound by no established or orthodox teachings or beliefs. Christ is pre-eminently a type of the universal. John the Baptist is a type of the personal. John dressed in a particular way, ate a particular kind of food, belonged to a particular order, lived and taught in a particular locality, and he himself recognized the fact that he must decrease while Christ must increase. Christ, on the other hand, gave Himself absolutely no limitations. He allowed Himself to be bound by nothing. He was absolutely universal and as a consequence taught not for His own particular day, but for all time.

This mighty truth which we have agreed upon as the great central fact of human life is the golden thread that runs through all religions. When we make it the paramount fact in our lives we shall find that minor differences, narrow prejudices, and all these laughable absurdities will so fall away by virtue of their very insignificance that a Jew can worship equally as well in a Catholic cathedral, a Catholic in a Jewish synagogue, a Buddhist in a Christian church, a Christian in a Buddhist temple. Or all can worship equally well about their own hearth-stones, or out on the hillside, or while pursuing the avocations of everyday life. For true worship, only God and the human soul are necessary. It does not depend upon times, or seasons, or occasions. Anywhere and at any time God and man in the bush may meet.

This is the great fundamental principle of the universal religion upon which all can agree. This is the great fact that is permanent. There are many things in regard to which all cannot agree. These are the things that are personal, non-essential, and so as time passes they gradually fall away. One who doesn't grasp this great truth, a Christian, for example, asks 'But was not Christ inspired?' Yes, but He was not the only one inspired. Another who is a Buddhist asks, 'Was not Buddha inspired?' Yes, but he was not the only one inspired. A Christian asks, 'But is not our Christian Bible inspired?' Yes, but there are other inspired scriptures. A Brahmin or a Buddhist asks, 'Are not the Vedas inspired?' Yes, but there are other inspired sacred books. Your error is not in believing that your particular scriptures are inspired, but your error is—and you show your absurdly laughable limitations by it—your inability to see that other scriptures are also inspired.

The sacred books, the inspired writings, all come from the same source —God, God speaking through the souls of those who open themselves that He may thus speak. Some may be more inspired than others. It depends entirely on the relative degree that this one or that one opens themselves to the Divine voice. Says one of the inspired writers in the Hebrew scriptures, Wisdom is the breath of the power of God, and in all ages entering into holy souls she maketh them friends of God and prophets.

Let us not be among the number so dwarfed, so limited, so bigoted as to think that the Infinite God has revealed Himself to one little handful of His children, in one little quarter of the globe, and at one particular period of time. This is not the pattern by which God works. Of a truth I perceive that God is no respecter of persons, but in every nation he that revereth God and worketh righteousness is accepted of Him, says the Christian Bible.

When we fully realize this truth we shall then see that it makes but little difference what particular form of religion one holds to, but it does make a tremendous difference how true he is to the vital principles of this one. In the degree that we love self less and love truth more, in that degree will we care less about converting people to our particular way of thinking, but all the more will we care to aid them in coming into the full realization of truth through the channels best adapted to them. The doctrine of our master, says the Chinese, consisted solely in integrity of heart. We shall find as we search that this is the doctrine of everyone who is at all worthy the name of master.

The great fundamental principles of all religions are the same. They differ only in their minor details according to the various degrees of unfoldment of different people. I am sometimes asked To what religion do you belong?' What religion? Why, bless you, there is only one religion, the 'religion of the living God!' There are, of course, the various creeds of the same religion arising from the various interpretations of different people, but they are all of minor importance. The more unfolded the soul the less important do these minor differences become. There are also, of course the various so-called religions. In reality, however, there is but one religion.

The moment we lose sight of this great fact we depart from the real, vital spirit of true religion and allow ourselves to be limited and bound by form. In the degree that we do this we build fences around ourselves which keep others away from us, and which also prevent our corning into the realization of universal truth; there is nothing worthy the name of truth that is not universal.

There is only one religion. 'Whatever road I take joins the highway that leads to Thee,' says the inspired writer in the Persian scriptures. 'Broad is the carpet God has spread, and beautiful the colors He has given it.' 'The pure man respects every form of faith,' says the Buddhist. 'My doctrine makes no difference between high and low, rich and poor, like the sky, it has room for all, and like the water, it washes all alike' The broad-minded see the truth in different religions; the narrow-minded see only the differences,' says the Chinese.

The Hindu has said, The narrow-minded ask, "Is this man a stranger, or is he of our tribe?" But to those in whom love dwells, the whole world is but one family.' 'Altar flowers are of many species, but all worship is one.' 'Heaven is a palace with many doors, and each may enter in his own way.' 'Are we not all children of one Father?' says the Christian. 'God has made of one blood all nations, to dwell on the face of the earth.' It was a latter-day seer who said, That which was profitable to the soul of man the Father revealed to the ancients; that which is profitable to the soul of man today revealeth He this day.'

It was Tennyson who said, 'I dreamed that stone by stone I reared a sacred fane, a temple, neither pagoda, mosque, nor church, but loftier, simpler, always open-doored to every breath from heaven, and Truth and Peace and Love and justice came and dwelt therein.'

Religion in its true sense is the most joyous thing the human soul can know, and when the real religion is realized we shall find that it will be an agent of peace, of joy, and of happiness, and never an agent of gloomy, long-faced sadness. It will then be attractive to all and repulsive to none. Let our Churches grasp these great truths, let them give their time and attention to bringing people into a knowledge of their true selves, into a knowledge of their relations, of their oneness, with the Infinite God, and such joy will be the result, and such crowds will flock to them, that their very walls will seem almost to burst, and such songs of joy will continually pour forth as will make all people in love with the religion that makes for everyday life, and hence the religion that is true and vital.

Adequacy for life, adequacy for everyday life here and now, must be the test of all true religion. If it does not bear this test, then it simply is not religion. We need an everyday, a this-world religion All time spent in connection with any other is worse than wasted. The eternal life that we are now living will be well loved if we take good care of each little period of time as it presents itself day after day. If we fail in doing this, we fail in everything.

Entering Now Into The Realization Of The Highest Riches

I hear the question, What can be said in a concrete way in regard to the method of coming into this realization? The facts underlying it are, indeed, most beautiful and true, but how can we actualize in ourselves the realization that carries with it such wonderful results?

The method is not difficult if we do not of ourselves make it difficult. The principal word to be used is the word — Open. Simply to open your mind and heart to this divine inflow which is waiting only for the opening of the gate, that it may enter. It is like opening the gate of the trough which conducts the water from the reservoir above into the field below. The water, by virtue of its very nature, will rush in and irrigate the field if the gate is but opened. As to the realization of our oneness with this Infinite Life and Power, after seeing, as I think we have clearly seen by this time, the relations it bears to us and we to it, the chief thing to be said is simply, Realize your oneness with it. The open mind and heart whereby one is brought into the receptive attitude is the first thing necessary. Then the earnest, sincere desire.

It may be an aid at first to take yourself for a few moments each day into the quiet, into the silence, where you will not be agitated by the disturbances that enter in through the avenues of the physical senses. There in the quiet alone with God, put yourself into the receptive attitude. Calmly, quietly, and expectantly desire that this realization break in upon and take possession of your soul. As it breaks in upon and takes possession of the soul, it will manifest itself to your mind, and from this you will feel its manifestations in every part of your body. Then in the degree that you open yourself to it you will feel a quiet, peaceful, illuminating power that will harmonize body, soul, and mind, and that will then harmonize these with all the world. You are now on the mountain top, and the voice of God is speaking to you. Then, as you descend, carry this realization with you. Live in it, waking, working, thinking, walking, sleeping. In this way, although you may not be continually on the mountain top, you will nevertheless be continually living in the realization of all the beauty, and inspiration, and power you have felt there.

Moreover, the time will come when in the busy office or the noisy street you can enter into the silence by simply drawing the mantle of your own thoughts about you and realizing that there and everywhere the Spirit of Infinite Life, Love, Wisdom, Peace, Power and Plenty is guiding, keeping, protecting, leading you. This is the spirit of continual prayer. This it is to pray without ceasing. This it is to know and to walk with God. This it is to find the Christ within. This is the new birth, the second birth. First that which is natural, then that which is spiritual. It is thus that the old man Adam is put off and the new man Christ is put on. This it is to be saved unto life eternal, whatever one's form of belief or faith may be; for it is life eternal to know God. 'The Sweet By and By' will be a song of the past. We shall create a new song: 'The Beautiful Eternal Now.'

This is the realization that you and I can come into this very day, this very hour, this very minute, if we desire and if we will it. And if now we merely set our faces in the right direction, it is then but a matter of time until we come into the full splendor of this complete realization. To set one's face in the direction of the mountain and then simply to journey on, whether rapidly or more slowly, will bring one to it. But unless one set their face in the right direction and make the start, they will not reach it. It was Goethe who said:

Are you in earnest? Seize this very minute:
What you can do, or dream you can, begin it.
Boldness has genius, power, and magic in it.
Only engage, and then the mind grows heated.
Begin, and then the work will be completed.

Said the young man, Gautama Siddhartha, I have awakened to the truth and I am resolved to accomplish my purpose. Verily I shall become a Buddha. It was this that brought him into the life of the Enlightened One, and so into the realization of Nirvana right here in this life. That this same realization and life is within the possibilities of all, here and now, was his teaching. It was this that has made him the Light Bearer to millions of people. Said the young man, Jesus, Know ye not that I must be about My Father's business? Making this the one great purpose of His life, He came into the full and complete realization—I and the Father are one. He thus came into the full realization of the Kingdom of Heaven right here in this life. That all could come into this same realization and life here and now was His teaching. It was this that has made Him the Light Bearer to millions of people.

And so far as practical things are concerned, we may hunt the wide universe through and we shall find that there is no injunction more practical than, Seek ye first the kingdom of God and His righteousness and all other things shall be added unto you. And in the light of what has gone before, I think there is no one who is open to truth and honest with themselves who will fail to grasp the underlying reason and see the great laws upon which it is based.

Personally I know lives that have so fully entered into the kingdom through the realization of their oneness with the Infinite Life, and through the opening of themselves so fully to its divine guidance, that they are most wonderful concrete examples of the reality of this great and all-important truth. They are people whose lives are in this way guided not only in the general way, but literally in every detail.

They simply live in the realization of their oneness with this Infinite Power, continually in harmony with it, and so continually in the realization of the kingdom of heaven. An abundance of all things is theirs. They are never at a loss for anything. The supply seems always equal to the demand. They never seem at a loss in regard to what to do or how to do it. Their lives are care-less lives. They are lives free from care because they are continually conscious of the fact that the higher powers are doing the guiding, and they are relieved of the responsibility.

To enter into detail in connection with some of these lives, and particularly with two or three that come to my mind at this moment, would reveal facts that no doubt to some would seem almost incredible, if not miraculous. But let us remember that what is possible for one life to realize is possible for all. This is indeed the natural and the normal life, that which will be the everyday life of everyone who comes into and who lives in this higher realization and so in harmony with the higher laws. This is simply getting into the current of that divine sequence running throughout the universe, and when once in it life then ceases to be a plodding, and moves along day after day much as the tides flow, much as the planets move in their courses, much as the seasons come and go.

All the frictions, all the uncertainties, all the ills, the sufferings, the fears, the forebodings, the perplexities of life come to us because we are out of harmony with the divine order of things. They will continue to come as long as we so live. Rowing against the tide is hard and uncertain. To go with the tide and thus to take advantage of the working of a great natural force is safe and easy. To come into the conscious, vital realization of our oneness with the Infinite Life and Power is to come into the current of this divine sequence. Coming thus into harmony with the Infinite brings us in turn into harmony with all about us, into harmony with the life of the heavens, into harmony with all the universe. And above all, it brings us into harmony with ourselves, so that body, soul, and mind become perfectly harmonized, and when this is so, life becomes full and complete.

The sense life then no longer masters and enslaves us. The physical is subordinated to and ruled by the mental; this in turn is subordinated to and continually illumined by the spiritual. Life is then no longer the poor, one-sided thing it is in so many cases; but the threefold, the all-round life with all its beauties and ever-increasing joys and powers is entered upon. Thus it is that we are brought to realize that the middle path is the great solution of life; neither asceticism on the one hand nor license and perverted use on the other. Everything is for use, but all must be wisely used in order to be fully enjoyed.

As we live in these higher realizations the senses are not ignored but are ever more fully perfected. As the body becomes less gross and heavy, finer in its texture and form, all the senses become finer, so that powers we do not now realize as belonging to us gradually develop. Thus we come, in a perfectly natural and normal way, into the super-conscious realms whereby we make it possible for the higher laws and truths to be revealed to us. As we enter into these realms we are then not among those who give their time in speculating as to whether this one or that one had the insight and the powers attributed to him, but we are able to know for ourselves. Neither are we among those who attempt to lead the people upon the hearsay of someone else, but we know whereof we speak, and only thus can we speak with authority.

There are many things that we cannot know until by living the life we bring ourselves into that state where it is possible for them to be revealed to us. 'If any man will do His will, he shall know of the doctrine.' It was Plotinus who said, The mind that wishes to behold God must itself become God. As we thus make it possible for these higher laws and truths to be revealed to us, we will in turn become enlightened ones, channels through which they may be revealed to others.

When one is fully alive to the possibilities that come with this higher awakening, as they go here and there, as they mingle with their fellow-man, they impart to all an inspiration that kindles in them a feeling of power kindred to their own. We are all continually giving out influences similar to those that are playing in our own lives. We do this in the same way that each flower emits its own peculiar odor. The rose breathes out its fragrance upon the air and all who come near it are refreshed and inspired by this emanation from the soul of the rose. A poisonous weed sends out its obnoxious odor; it is neither refreshing nor inspiring in its effects, and if one remain near it long they may be so unpleasantly affected as to be made even ill by it.

The higher the life the more inspiring and helpful are the emanations that it is continually sending out. The lower the life the more harmful is the influence it continually sends out to all who come in contact with it. Each one is continually radiating an atmosphere of one kind or the other.

We are told by the mariners who sail on the Indian Seas that many times they are able to tell their approach to certain islands, long before they can see them, by the sweet fragrance of the sandalwood that is wafted far out upon the deep. Do you not see how it would serve to have such a soul playing through such a body that as you go here and there a subtle, silent force goes out from you that all feel and are influenced by; so that you carry with you an inspiration and continually shed a benediction wherever you go; so that your friends and all people will say, his coming brings peace and joy into our homes, welcome his coming; so that as you pass along the street, tired, and weary, and even sin-sick men will feel a certain divine touch that will awaken new desires and a new life in them; that will make the very horse, as you pass him, turn his head with a strange, half-human, longing look? Such are the subtle powers of the human soul when it makes itself translucent to the Divine. To know that such a life is within our living here and now is enough to make one burst forth with songs of joy. And when the life itself is entered upon, the sentiment of at least one song will be:

Oh! I stand in the Great Forever,
All things to me are divine,
I eat of the heavenly manna,
I drink of the heavenly wine.
In the gleam of the shining rainbow
The Fathers Love I behold,
As I gaze on its radiant blending
Of crimson and blue and gold.
In all the bright birds that are singing,
In all the fair flowers that bloom,
Whose welcome aromas are bringing
Their blessings of sweet perfume.
In the glorious tint of the morning,
In the gorgeous sheen of the night,
Oh! my soul is lost in rapture,
My senses are lost in sight.

When one comes into and lives continually in the full, conscious realization of oneness with the Infinite Life and Power, then all else follows. This it is that brings the realization of such splendors, and beauties, and joys as a life that is thus related with the Infinite Power alone can know. This it is to come into the realization of heaven's richest treasures while walking the earth. This it is to bring heaven down to earth, or rather to bring earth up to heaven. This it is to exchange weakness and impotence for strength; sorrows and sighings for joy; fears and forebodings for faith; longings for realizations. This it is to come into fullness of peace, power, and plenty. This it is to be in tune with the Infinite.

"The Way"

Life is not so complex if we do not so persistently make it so. We accept the results or the effects; but we concern ourselves all too little with the realm of cause. The springs of life are all from within. Invariably it is true —as is the inner so always and inevitably will be the outer.

There is a Divine current that will bear us with peace and safety on its bosom if we are sufficiently alert and determined to find it—and go with it. The natural, normal life is by a law divine under the guidance of the Spirit.

There is a mystic force that transcends the powers of the intellect and likewise of the body. There are certain faculties that we have that are not a part of the active, thinking mind; they transcend any possible activities of the active, thinking mind. Through them we have intuitions, impulses, leadings, that instead of being merely the occasional, should be the normal and habitual.

They would be if we understood better the laws that pertain to them and observed them; for here, as in connection with everything in the universe and everything in human life, all is governed by law —the Elemental law of cause and effect. Supreme Intelligence, Creative Power, works only through law. There is an inner spirit or guide that rules and regulates the life when the life is brought into that state or condition whereby it can make itself known, and in turn dominate the life.

Jesus, Master of the laws of life, and supreme revealer of them to men, had a full and practical knowledge of it. He not only abundantly demonstrated it in His own life; but He made clear the way whereby it may become the common possession of other lives. Do not worry about your life, was the Master's clear-cut and repeated command. He not only gave the injunction or command, but He demonstrated the method whereby the fears and forebodings and uncertainties of life can be displaced by a force or a power that will bring them to an end.

It was embodied in His other injunction or command that He gave utterance to so repeatedly: 'Seek ye first the Kingdom of God and His righteousness and all these things shall be added to you.' And by all these things, He meant, all of the common needs and necessities of the daily life.

The finding of the Kingdom of God is the recognition of the indwelling Divine Life as the source, and therefore as the Essence, of our own lives. It is the bringing of men's minds and therefore acts into harmony with the Divine will and purpose. It is the saving of men from their lower conceptions and selves, and a lifting them up to a realization of their higher selves, which, as He taught, is eternally one with God, the Father; and which, when realized, lifts a man's thoughts, acts, purposes, and conduct —his entire life —up to that pattern or standard.

It was not merely a poetic fancy, but the recognition of a fundamental law, as well-known laws of modern psychology, mental and spiritual science, are now clearly demonstrating, that induced the Master to say: 'And thine ears shall hear a word behind thee, saying, This is the way, walk ye in it, when ye turn to the right-hand and when ye turn to the left.' And again: 'The Lord in the midst of thee is mighty.' And still again: 'He that dwelleth in the secret place of the Most High shall abide under the shadow of the Almighty.'

How often do the meager accounts of the Master's life tell us of His going up to the mountain to pray for communion with the Father. And then we find Him invariably down among men, always where the need for help and for human service was the greatest.

This habit of taking a little time daily alone, in the quiet, in communion with one's Source that the illumination and guidance of the Holy Spirit may become alive and active in the life, and going then about one's daily work ever open to and conscious of this Divine guidance, trusting and resting in it, strengthened and sustained always by this Divine power, will bring definiteness and direction, will bring hope and courage, will bring peace and power to everyone who will heed the Master's injunction and will follow His example. These it has brought to great numbers to whom before, life was an enigma, and this because the life had been lived entirely from the outside.

The higher forces and powers of the inner life, those of the mind and spirit, always potential within, become of actual value only as they are recognized, realized, and used. The Master's Way of the Spirit, the finding of the Kingdom within, leads in to no blind alley. It leads out and triumphantly out on to the great plain of clear vision, of un-self-centered activity, of heroic endeavor and accomplishment.

If we would spend a fraction of the time that we spend in needless anxiety in definite constructive thought, in 'silent demand', visualizing the conditions that we would have, with faith in their fulfillment, we would soon know that the Master's illustration of the care-free bird is fact and not fancy. It is, He said, what life should be.

The little time spent in the quiet each day, alone with one's God, that we may make and keep our connection with the Infinite Source—our source and our life—will be a boon to any life. It will prove, if we are faithful, to be the most priceless possession that we have.

While it is impossible for one to make a formula which another should follow, the following may perchance contain some little suggestions —each must follow his or her own leading and, therefore, method.

My Father in Heaven, Infinite Spirit of life and love and wisdom and power, in whom I live and move and have my being, whence cometh my help, manifest Thyself in me.

Help me to open myself to the highest wisdom and insight and love and power, that I may serve Thee and my fellow-man, and all my fellow-creatures faithfully, and that I may have the Divine guidance and care, and that all my needs be supplied.

Oh Christ within, enfold and lead me and reign supreme, that the One Life that is my life I may realize and manifest ever more fully. I am strong in the Infinite Spirit of life and love and wisdom and power. I have and shall have the Divine guidance and care; for it is the Father that worketh in me —My Father works and I work.

A Resolve For Today

The following little motto — a resolve for today — may contain a little aid for the following of the Way.

I Am Resolved
I believe that my Master intended that I take His teachings in the simple, frank, and open manner in which He gave them, out on the hill-side, by the calm blue waters of the Galilean sea, and out under the stars of heaven.

I believe that He knew what He meant, and that He meant what He said, when He gave the substance of all religion and the duty of man as love to God, and love and service for His fellow-man.

I am therefore resolved at this, the beginning of another day, this fresh beginning of life, to go forth eager and happy and unafraid, in that I can come into the same filial relations of love and guidance and care with my Father in Heaven that my Master realized and lived, and going before revealed to me.

I shall listen intently to know, and shall run with eager feet to do my Father's will, calm and quiet within, knowing that I shall have the Divine guidance and care, and that no harm therefore shall befall me; for I am now living in God's life and there I shall live forever.

I am resolved in all human contact to meet petulance with patience, questionings with kindness, hatred with love, eager always to do the kindly deed that brings the joy of service—and that alone makes human life truly human. I shall seek no advantage for myself to the detriment or the harm of my neighbor, knowing that it is only through the law of mutuality that I can fully enjoy what I gain—or can even be a man.

I am resolved therefore so to live this day that, when the twilight comes and the night falls, I shall be not only another day's journey nearer home; but I shall have lived a man's part and done a man's work in the world and shall indeed deserve my Father's love and care.

Thoughts I Met On the Highway

Thoughts are forces—like builds like and like attracts like. Thoughts of strength both build strength from within and attract it from without. Thoughts of weakness actualize weakness from within and attract it from without. Courage begets strength, fear begets weakness. And so courage begets success, fear begets failure.

Any way the old world goes
Happy be the weather!
With the red thorn or the rose
Singin' all together!
Don't you see that sky o' blue!
Good Lord painted it for you

Reap the daisies in the dew
Singin' all together!
Springtime sweet, an' frosty fall
Happy be the weather!
Earth has gardens for us all,
Goin' on together.

Sweet the labor in the light,
To the harvest's gold and white—
Till the toilers say "Good night,"
Singin' all together!

There is no quality that exerts more good, is of greater service to all mankind during the course of the ordinary life, than the mind and the heart that goes out in an all-embracing love for all, that is the generator and the circulator of a genuine, hearty, wholesome sympathy and courage and good cheer, that is not disturbed or upset by the passing occurrence little or great, but that is serene, tranquil, and conquering to the end, that is looking for the best, that is finding the best, and that is inspiring the best in all. There is moreover, no quality that when genuine brings such rich returns to its possessor by virtue of the thoughts and the feelings that it inspires and calls forth from others and that come back laden with their peaceful, stimulating, healthful influences for you.

Out of the night that covers me,
Black as the Pit from pole to pole,
I thank whatever gods may be
For my unconquerable soul.

In the fell clutch of circumstance
I have not winced nor cried aloud.
Under the bludgeoning of chance
My head is bloody, but unbowed.

Beyond this place of wrath and tears
Looms but the horror of the shade,
And yet the menace of the years
Finds and shall find me, unafraid.

It matters not how strait the gate
How charged with punishment the scroll,
I am the master of my fate;
I am the captain of my soul.—*William Earnest Henley*

Thought is the great builder in human life: it is the determining factor. Continually think thoughts that are good, and your life will show forth in goodness, and your body in health and beauty. Continually think evil thoughts, and your life will show forth in evil, and your body in weakness and repulsiveness. Think thoughts of love, and you will love and will be loved. Think thoughts of hatred, and you will hate and will be hated. Each follows its kind.

Every day is a fresh beginning,
Every morning is the world made new;
You who are weary of sorrow and sinning,
Here is a beautiful hope for you,
A hope for me and a hope for you.

All the past things are past and over,
The tasks are done, and the tears are shed.
Yesterday's errors let yesterday cover;
Yesterday's wounds, which smarted and bled,
Are healed with the healing which night has shed.

Every day is a fresh beginning,
Listen, my soul, to the glad refrain,
And, spite of old sorrow and older sinning,
And puzzles forecasted, and possible pain,
Take heart with the day and begin again.

Each morning is a fresh beginning. We are, as it were, just beginning life. We have it *entirely* in our own hands. And when the morning with its fresh beginning comes, all yesterdays should be yesterdays, with which we have nothing to do. Sufficient is it to know that the way we lived our yesterday has determined for us our today. And, again, when the morning with its fresh beginning comes, all tomorrows should be tomorrows, with which we have nothing to do. Sufficient to know that the way we live our today determines our tomorrow.

Simply the first hour of this new day, with all its richness and glory, with all its sublime and eternity-determining possibilities, and each succeeding hour as it comes, but *not before* it comes—this is the secret of character building. This simple method will bring any one to the realization of the highest life that can be even conceived of, and there is nothing in this connection that can be conceived of that cannot be realized somehow, somewhen, somewhere.

> The poem hangs on the berry-bush
> When comes the poet's eye,
> And the whole street is a masquerade
> When Shakespeare passes by.

This same Shakespeare, whose mere passing causes all this commotion, is the one who put into the mouth of one of his creations the words: "The fault, dear Brutus, is not in our stars, but in ourselves, that we are underlings." And again he gave us a great truth when he said:

> "Our doubts are traitors,
> And make us lose the good we oft might win
> By fearing to attempt."

There is probably no agent that brings us more undesirable conditions than fear. We should live in fear of nothing, nor will we when we come fully to know ourselves. An old French proverb runs:

> "Some of your griefs you have cured,
> And the sharpest you still have survived;
> But what torments of pain you endured
> From evils that never arrived."

Fear and lack of faith go hand in hand. The one is born of the other. Tell me how much one is given to fear, and I will tell you how much he lacks in faith. Fear is a most expensive guest to entertain, the same as worry is: so expensive are they that no one can afford to entertain them. We invite what we fear, the same as, by a different attitude of mind, we invite and attract the influences and conditions we desire.

To remain in nature always sweet and simple and humble, and therefore strong.

> "Whatever the weather may be," says he,
> "Whatever the weather may be,
> It's the songs ye sing, an' the smiles ye wear,

That's a-makin' the sun shine everywhere."—*James Whitcomb Riley*

Sweetness of nature, simplicity in manners and conduct, humility without self-abasement, give the truly kingly quality to men, the queenly to women, the winning to children, whatever the rank or the station may be. The life dominated by this characteristic, or rather these closely allied characteristics, is a natural well-spring of joy to itself and sheds a continual benediction upon all who come within the scope of its influence. It makes for a life of great beauty in itself, and it imparts courage and hope and buoyancy to all others.

There is no thing we cannot overcome;
Say not thy evil instinct is inherited,
Or that some trait inborn makes thy whole life forlorn;
And calls down punishment that is not merited.

Back of thy parents and grandparents lies
The Great Eternal Will! That too is thine
Inheritance,—strong, beautiful, divine,
Sure lever of success for one who tries.

Earth has no claim the soul cannot contest;
Know thyself part of the Eternal Source;
Naught can stand before thy spirit's force:
The soul's Divine Inheritance is best.

Thought is at the bottom of all progress or retrogression, of all success or failure, of all that is desirable or undesirable in human life. The type of thought we entertain both creates and draws conditions that crystallize about it, conditions exactly the same in nature as is the thought that gives them form. Thoughts are forces, and each creates of its kind, whether we realize it or not. The great law of the drawing power of the mind, which says that like creates like, and that like attracts like, is continually working in every human life, for it is one of the great immutable laws of the universe. For one to take time to see clearly the things one would attain to, and then to hold that ideal steadily and continually before his mind, never allowing faith—his positive thought-forces—to give way to or to be neutralized by doubts and fears, and then to set about doing each day what his hands find to do, never complaining, but spending the time that he would otherwise spend in complaint in focusing his thought-forces upon the ideal that his mind has built, will sooner or later bring about the full materialization of that for which he sets out.

Beauty seen is never lost,
God's colors all are fast;

> The glory of this sunset heaven
> Into my soul has passed,—
> A sense of gladness unconfined
> To mortal, date or clime;
> As the soul liveth, it shall live
> Beyond the years of time.
> Beside the mystic asphodels
> Shall bloom the home-born flowers,
> And new horizons flush and glow
> With sunset hues of ours. —*Whittier*

Would you remain always young, and would you carry all the joyousness and buoyancy of youth into your maturer years? Then have care concerning but one thing,—how you live in your thought world. It was the inspired one, Gautama, the Buddha, who said,—"The mind is everything; what you think you become." And the same thing had Ruskin in mind when he said,—"Make yourselves nests of pleasant thoughts. None of us as yet know, for none of us have been taught in early youth, what fairy palaces we may build of beautiful thought—*proof against all adversity*." And would you have in your body all the elasticity, all the strength, all the beauty of your younger years? Then live these in your mind, making no room for unclean thought, and you will externalize them in your body. In the degree that you keep young in thought will you remain young in body. And you will find that your body will in turn aid your mind, for body helps mind the same as mind helps body.

> There is a sacred Something on all ways—
> Something that watches through the Universe;
> One that remembers, reckons and repays,
> Giving us love for love, and curse for curse. —*Edwin Markham*

The power of every life, the very life itself, is determined by what it relates itself to. God is immanent as well as transcendent. He is creating, working, ruling in the universe today, in your life and in mine, just as much as He ever has been. We are too apt to regard Him after the manner of an absentee landlord, one who has set in operation the forces of this great universe, and then taken Himself away.

In the degree, however, that we recognize Him as immanent as well as transcendent, are we able to partake of His life and power. For in the degree that we recognize Him as the Infinite Spirit of Life and Power that is today, at this very moment, working and manifesting in and through all, and then, in the degree that we come into the realization of our oneness with this life, do we become partakers of, and so do we actualize in ourselves the qualities of his life. In the degree that we open ourselves to the inflowing tide of this immanent and transcendent life, do we make ourselves channels through which the Infinite Intelligence and Power can work.

> The robber is robbed by his riches;
> The tyrant is dragged by his chain;
> The schemer is snared by his cunning,
> The slayer lies dead by the slain.—*Edwin Markham*

This is the law of prosperity: When apparent adversity comes, be not cast down by it, but make the best of it, and always look forward for better things, for conditions more prosperous. To hold yourself in this attitude of mind is to set into operation subtle, silent, and irresistible forces that sooner or later will actualize in material form that which is today merely an idea. But ideas have occult power, and ideas, when rightly planted and rightly tended, are the seeds that actualize material conditions.

Never give a moment to complaint, but utilize the time that would otherwise be spent in this way in looking forward and actualizing the conditions you desire. Suggest prosperity to yourself. See yourself in a prosperous condition. Affirm that you will before long be in a prosperous condition. Affirm it calmly and quietly, but strongly and confidently. Believe it, believe it absolutely. Expect it,—keep it continually watered with expectation. You thus make yourself a magnet to attract the things that you desire. Don't be afraid to suggest.

> They might not need me—yet they might,
> I'll let my heart be just in sight.
> A smile so small as mine might be
> Precisely their necessity. —*Emily Dickinson*

The grander natures and the more thoughtful are always looking for and in conversation dwelling on the better things in others. It is the rule with but few, if any exceptions, that the more noble and worthy and thoughtful the nature, the more it is continually looking for the best there is to be found in every life. Instead of judging or condemning, or acquiring the habit that eventually leads to this, it is looking more closely to and giving its time to living more worthily itself.

It is in this way continually unfolding and expanding in beauty and in power; it is finding an ever-increasing happiness by the admiration and the love that such a life is always, even though all unconsciously, calling to itself from all sources. It is the life that pays by many fold.

> We just shake hands at meeting
> With many that come nigh
> We nod the head in greeting
> To many that go by—

But welcome through the gateway
Our few old friends and true;
Then hearts leap up, and straightway
There's open house for you.
Old friends.
There's open house for you! —*Gerald Massey*

Many times the struggles are greater than we can ever know. We need more gentleness and sympathy and compassion in our common human life. Then we will neither blame nor condemn. Instead of blaming or condemning we will sympathize.

"Comfort one another.
For the way is often dreary
And the feet are often weary,
And the heart is very sad.
There is a heavy burden bearing,
When it seems that none are caring,
And we half forget that ever we were glad.

"Comfort one another
With the hand-clasp close and tender.
With the sweetness love can render,
And the looks of friendly eyes.
Do not wait with grace unspoken,
While life's daily bread is broken—
Gentle speech is oft like manna from the skies."

And then when we fully realize the fact that selfishness is at the root of all error, sin, and crime, and that ignorance is the basis of all selfishness, with what charity we come to look upon the acts of all. It is the ignorant man who seeks his own ends at the expense of the greater whole. It is the ignorant man, therefore, who is the selfish man.

To get up immediately when we stumble, face again to the light, and travel on without wasting even a moment in regret.

We are on the way from the imperfect to the perfect; some day, in this life or some other, we shall reach our destiny. It is as much the part of folly to waste time and cripple our forces in vain, unproductive regrets in regard to the occurences of the past as it is to cripple our forces through fears and forebodings for the future.

There is no experience in any life which if rightly recognized, rightly turned and thereby wisely used, cannot be made of value; many times things thus turned and used can be made sources of inestimable gain; ofttimes they become veritable blessings in disguise.

> 'Tis the sweetest thing to remember
> If courage be on the wane.
> When the cold, dark days are over—
> Why, the birds go north again.—*Ella Higginson*

Nothing is more subtle than thought, nothing more powerful, nothing more irresistible in its operations, when rightly applied and held to with a faith and fidelity that is unswerving,—a faith and fidelity that never knows the neutralizing effects of doubt and fear. If one have aspirations and a sincere desire for a higher and better condition, so far as advantages, facilities, associates, or any surroundings or environments are concerned, and if he continually send out his highest thought forces for the realization of these desires, and continually water these forces with firm expectation as to their fulfillment, he will sooner or later find himself in the realization of these desires, and all in accordance with natural laws and forces.

We are born to be neither slaves nor beggars, but to dominion and to plenty. This is our rightful heritage, if we will but recognize and lay claim to it.

> One who never turned his back, but marched breast forward,
> Never doubted clouds would break,
> Never dreamed, though right were worsted, wrong would triumph,
> Held we fall to rise, are baffled to fight better,
> Sleep to wake.—*Robert Browning*

Will is the steady directing power: it is concentration. It is the pilot which, after the vessel is started by the mighty force within, puts it on its right course and keeps it true to that course.

Will is the sun-glass which so concentrates and so focuses the sun's rays that they quickly burn a hole through the paper that is held before it. The same rays, not thus concentrated, not thus focused, would fall upon the paper for days without any effect whatever. Will is the means for the directing, the concentrating, the focusing, of the thought-forces. Thought under wise direction,—this it is that does the work, that brings results, that makes the successful career. One object in mind which we never lose sight of; an ideal steadily held before the mind, never lost sight of, never lowered, never swerved from,—this, with *persistence*, determines all. Nothing can resist the power of thought, when thus directed by will.

> To stand by one's friend to the uttermost end,
> And fight a fair fight with one's foe;
> Never to quit and never to twit,
> And never to peddle one's woe. —*George Brinton Chandler*

The fearing, grumbling, worrying, vascillating do not succeed in anything and generally live by burdening, in some form or another, someone else. They stand in the way of, they prevent their own success; they fail in living even an ordinary healthy, normal life; they cast a blighting influence over and they act as a hindrance to all with whom they at any time come in contact. The pleasures we take captive in life, the growth and advancement we make, the pleasure and benefit our company or acquaintanceship brings to others, the very desirability of our companionship on the part of others—all depend upon the types of thought we entertain and live most habitually with.

No one could tell me where my Soul might be.
I searched for God but God eluded me.
I sought my brother out and found all there.—*Ernest Crosby*.

In the degree that we love will we be loved. Thoughts are forces. Each creates of its kind. Each comes back laden with the effect that corresponds to itself and of which it is the cause.

"Then let your secret thoughts be fair—
They have a vital part, and share
In shaping words and moulding fate;
God's system is so intricate."

If our heart goes out in love to all with whom we come in contact, we inspire love and the same ennobling and warming influences of love always return to us from those in whom we inspire them. There is a deep scientific principle underlying the precept—If you would have all the world love you, you must first love all the world.

It was only a glad "Good morning!"
As she passed along the way,
But it spread the morning glory
Over the livelong day.

By example and not by precept. By living, not by preaching. By doing, not by professing. By living the life, not by dogmatizing as to how it should be lived. There is no contagion equal to the contagion of life. Whatever we sow, that shall we also reap, and each thing sown produces of its kind. We can kill not only by doing another bodily injury directly, but we can and we do kill by every antagonistic thought. Not only do we thus kill, but while we kill we suicide. Many a man has been made sick by having the ill thoughts of a number of people centered upon him; some have been actually killed. Put hatred into the world and we make it a literal hell. Put love into the world and heaven with all its beauties and glories becomes a reality.

Not to love is not to live, or it is to live a living death. The life that goes out in love to all is the life that is full, and rich, and continually expanding in beauty and in power. Such is the life that becomes ever more inclusive, and hence larger in its scope and influence.

Give us men!
Strong and stalwart ones:
Men whom highest hope inspires,
Men whom purest honour fires,
Men who trample Self beneath them.
Men who make their country wreathe them
As her noble sons,
Worthy of their sires,
Men who never shame their mothers,
Men who never fail their brothers,
True, however false are others:
Give us Men—I say again,
Give us Men!—*The Bishop of Exeter*

Not repression, but elevation. Would that this could be repeated a thousand times over! *No, a knowledge of the spiritual realities of life prohibits asceticism, repression, the same as it prohibits license and perverted use. To err on the one side is just as contrary to the ideal life as to err on the other.* All things are for a purpose, all should be used and enjoyed; but all should be rightly used, that they may be fully enjoyed.

It is the all-around, fully developed we want,—not the ethereal, pale-blooded man and woman, but the man and woman of flesh and blood, for action and service here and now,—the man and woman strong and powerful, with all the faculties and functions fully unfolded and used, all in a royal and bounding condition, but all rightly subordinated. The man and the woman of this kind, with the imperial hand of mastery upon all,—standing, moving thus like a king, nay, like a very God,—such is the man and such is the woman of power. Such is the ideal life: anything else is one-sided, and falls short of it.

High thought and noble in all lands
Help me; my soul is fed by such,
But oh, at the touch of life and hands—
The human touch!
Warm, vital, close, life's Symbol dear,—
These need I most, and now and here.—*Richard Burton*

Thoughts of strength both build strength from within and attract it from without. Thoughts of weakness actualize weakness from within and attract it from without. Courage begets strength, fear begets weakness. And so courage begets success, fear begets failure. It is the man or the woman of faith, and hence of courage, who is the master of circumstances, and who make his or her power felt in the world. It is the man or the woman who lacks faith and who as a consequence is weakened and crippled by fears and forebodings, who is the creature of all passing occurences.

What one lives in his invisible thought world he is continually actualizing in his visible material world. If he would have any conditions different in the latter he must make the necessary change in the former. A clear realization of this great fact would bring success to thousands of men and women who all about us are now in the depths of despair. It would bring health, abounding health and strength to thousands now diseased and suffering. It would bring peace and joy to thousands now unhappy and ill at ease.

I stay my haste, I make delays,
For what avails this eager pace?
I stand amid eternal ways,
And what is mine shall know my face

Asleep, awake, by night or day,
The friends I seek are seeking me;
No wind can drive my bark astray,
Nor change the tide of destiny—

The waters know their own, and draw
The brooks that spring in yonder height;
So flows the good with equal law
Unto the soul of pure delight.

The stars come nightly to the sky;
The tidal wave unto the sea;
Nor time, nor space, nor deep, nor high,
Can keep my own away from me.—*John Burroughs*

The thing that pays, and that makes for a well balanced, useful, and happy life, is not necessarily and is not generally a somber, pious morality, or any standard of life that keeps us from a free, happy, spontaneous use and enjoyment of all normal and healthy faculties, functions, and powers, the enjoyment of all innocent pleasures—use, but not abuse, enjoyment, but enjoyment through self-mastery and not through license or perverted use, for it can never come that way. Look where we will, in or out and around us, we will find that it is the middle ground—neither poverty nor excessive riches, good wholesome use without license, a turning into the bye-ways along the main road where innocent and healthy God-sent and God-intended pleasures and enjoyments are to be found; but never getting far enough away to lose sight of the road itself. The middle ground it is that the wise man or woman plants foot upon.

>   For evil poisons; malice shafts
>   Like boomerangs return,
>   Inflicting wounds that will not heal
>   While rage and anger burn.

Tell me how much one loves and I will tell you how much he has seen of God. Tell me how much he loves and I will tell you how much he lives with God. Tell me how much he loves and I will tell you how far into the Kingdom of Heaven,—the kingdom of harmony, he has entered, for "love is the fulfilling of the law."

And in a sense love is everything. It is the key to life, and its influences are those that move the world. Live only in the thought of love for all and you will draw love to you from all. Live in the thought of malice or hatred, and malice and hatred will come back to you.

And so love inspires love; hatred breeds hatred. Love and good will stimulate and build up the body; hatred and malice corrode and tear it down. Love is a savor of life unto life; hatred is a savor of death unto death.

>   "There are loyal hearts, there are spirits brave,
>   There are souls that are pure and true;
>   Then give to the world the best you have,
>   And the best will come back to you.
>
>   "Give love, and love to *your* heart will flow,
>   A strength in your utmost need;
>   Have faith, and a score of hearts will show
>   Their faith in *your* word and deed."

>   The kind of a man for you and me!
>   He faces the world unflinchingly,
>   And smiles as long as the world exists,
>   With a knuckled faith and force like fists:
>   He lives the life he is preaching of,
>   And loves where most is the need of love;
>   And feeling still, with a grief half glad,
>   That the bad are as good as the good are bad,
>   He strikes straight out for the right—and he
>   Is the kind of a man for you and me!—*James Whitcomb Riley*

After a certain age is reached in any life, the prevailing tone and condition of that life is the resultant of the mental habits of that life. If one have mental equipment sufficient to find and to make use of the Science of Thought in its application to scientific mind and body building, habit and character building, there is little by way of heredity, environment, attainment of which he or she will not be the master.

One thing is very certain—the mental points of view, the mental tendencies and habits at twenty-eight and thirty-eight will have externalized themselves and will have stamped the prevailing conditions of any life at forty-eight and fifty-eight and sixty-eight.

> Who puts back into place a fallen bar.
> Or flings a rock out of a traveled road,
> His feet are moving toward the central star,
> His name is whispered in the Gods' abode.—*Edwin Markham*

We need changes from the duties and the cares of our accustomed everyday life. They are necessary for healthy, normal living. We need occasionally to be away from our friends, our relatives, from the members of our immediate households. Such changes are good for us; they are good for them. We appreciate them better, they us, when we are away from them for a period, or they from us.

We need these changes to get the kinks out of our minds, our nerves, our muscles—the cobwebs off our faces. We need them to whet again the edge of appetite. We need them to invite the mind and the soul to new possibilities and powers. We need them in order to come back with new implements, or with implements redressed, sharpened, for the daily duties.

We need periods of being by ourselves—*alone*. Sometimes a fortnight or even a week will do wonders for one, unless he or she has drawn too heavily upon the account. The simple custom, moreover, of taking an hour, or even a half hour, *alone in the quiet*, in the midst of the daily routine of life, would be the source of *inestimable gain* for countless numbers.

> I know not where His islands lift
> Their fronded palms in air;
> I only know I cannot drift
> Beyond His love and care.—*Whittier*

We need more faith in everyday life—faith in the power that works for good, faith in the Infinite God, and hence faith in ourselves created in His image. And however things at times may seem to go, however dark at times appearances may be, the knowledge of the fact that "the Supreme Power has us in its charge as it has the suns and endless systems of worlds in space," will give us the supreme faith that all is well with us, the same as all is well with the world. "Thou wilt keep him in perfect peace whose mind is stayed on Thee."

There is nothing firmer, and safer, and surer than Deity. Then, as we recognize the fact that we have it in our own hands to open ourselves ever more fully to this Infinite Power, and call upon it to manifest itself in and through us, we will find in ourselves an ever increasing sense of power. For in this way we are working in conjunction with it, and it in turn is working in conjunction with us. We are then led into the full realization of the fact that all things work together for good to those that love the good.

Earth breaks up, time drops away,
In flows Heaven with its new day.—*Browning*

www.ingramcontent.com/pod-product-compliance
Lightning Source LLC
Chambersburg PA
CBHW031647040426
42453CB00006B/241